James W

Illustrations by Ste

HIT

Once Upon a Field

First published in 2023
Walker & Company Publishing

© James Walker 2023

ISBN 978-1-7393803-0-4
ISBN 978-1-7393803-1-1

Walker & Company
Catalogue number // 001

Cover image: Stephen Reding, Self-portrait in a Spoon (2006)

Contents

Prologue	Time is Flying	1
1	Seven Miles Out	5
2	Once Upon a Family	9
3	Northern Lights	17
4	Hit	31
5	Picking up the Pieces	33
6	A Portrait of the Young Man as an Artist	41
7	Brainwave	55
8	Ōm̐	73
9	Going Solo	77
10	Human Traffic	83
11	Somniferum	93
12	Searching for Stephen	95
13	Paradise Lost	107
14	Travelling at the Speed of Dark	121
15	Buried Treasure	137
16	Low	157
17	Memories of the Future	165
18	Back to Life	173
19	Infinitum	183
20	The Tide Will Sway	201
21	After Image	203
22	Back in Black	209
23	Once Upon a Field	217
24	Rise	221
Epilogue	Painting the Artist	237
	End Notes	249
	Acknowledgements	251
	About the Author	253

paintingtheartist.com

The names of some individuals have been changed

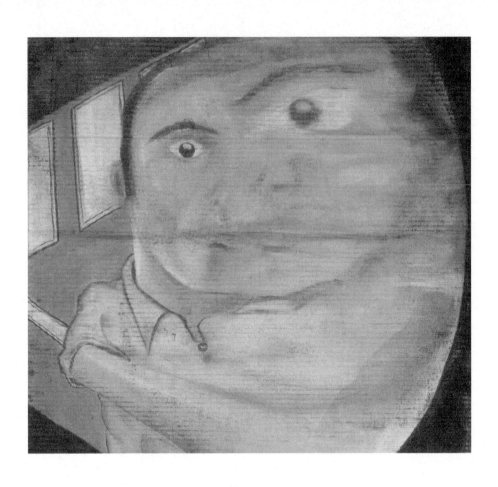

Self-portrait in a Blue Room (2006)
Chalk pastel, charcoal pencil

For Mary

Metropolis (2004)
Oil paint on canvas

HIT

Once Upon a Field

James Walker

Illustrations by Stephen Reding

Walker & Company

Ko Pha Ngan (2000)
Pen and ink, watercolour

Water is Life and Heaven's Gift
Here Rivers Goyt and Tame Become Mersey
Flowing Clear From Stockport to the Sea[1]

Untitled 67 (2006)
Oil paint on canvas

Time is Flying

THE SUN HAD ALREADY passed its peak on that March afternoon. It shone down through the window of the old public house, cast a triangle on the table, and danced around the smoky room. The usual lunchtime bustle came from all corners: huddled recollections of last night's escapades, intermittent explosions of laughter, the occasional clink of cutlery. Punters were sinking pints to make room for one more. *My round next, lads… What was I saying?* The stone-tiled floor was already feeling that Saturday sway.

I remember that day completely.

We sat in an alcove by the bay window of *The George*. Stephen had been talking for more than an hour. His eyes were wide. He barely stopped to take a breath, but finally caught himself mid-sentence.

—I'm sorry, James.

He settled back into his chair and knocked the foam from his beer. His voice was tense, excited. *I'm sorry.* Those words repeated over and over, as Stephen went deeper into his story, deeper into his past. White paint flecked his hands and flashed in the sun as he spoke.

To this day, I'm still not sure exactly what Stephen was apologising for. He'd certainly caused me no harm. It was true that my cousin had been through a dark period, but he was now getting his life back on track. He was on the cusp of completing a 12-month methadone programme, and soon his daily dose would be reduced to zero. More importantly, he had become immersed in his art once again.

I sometimes wonder whether Stephen's constant apologies came in response to my own reactions. He was telling me things that no one else knew, events he'd never spoken of before. And I *was* shocked. My eyes were probably wider than his. But no apologies were needed. I wanted to hear more. I wanted to hear everything. I took a pinch of his tobacco and urged him to continue.

§

My cousin had travelled the long road to get to where he was now. The preceding years had seen him come in and out of our lives sporadically – from going missing in Southeast Asia to being absent on our own shores. But now, as with everyone else in the family, I was just glad to have him back. He was the closest person I had to an older brother, and it was the first time the two of us had met together, alone, since his return. It felt good, and more so because it was clear that heroin no longer held a grip on his life. It was a small pleasure simply to walk around our old stomping ground after so many years, tracing the pathways and the alleyways and the places where we used to play.

That afternoon, Stephen told me things I couldn't have imagined in my wildest dreams. This unrehearsed monologue was the stuff of movies. These weren't the kind of things that happened to a normal lad from the suburbs of Manchester. He grew increasingly animated as he recounted tale after tale, episode after episode. Synapses flashed among remembered situations. Neurons exploded like fireworks over the memories of a not-too-distant life.

As I listened to him talk, I hadn't noticed the slow transition of the pub's clientele from the lunching weekend workers to groups of men and women who were clearly in for the long haul. The tone had shifted up a notch.

—Come on, we'd best get going.

We placed our empty glasses at the end of the bar and left through the old oak doors.

§

Stephen was painting again. I guess he never *really* stopped. But now, after having been clean for nearly a year, he was creating bigger and bolder pieces than ever before. In the months since his return to his family - to his life - he was producing fresh paintings at a rapid pace, trying out new ideas with increasing ambition. His new flat, on the outskirts of Stockport, was perhaps best described as an artist's studio with a bed. There were paint tubes and canvasses strewn all around; paintbrushes and easels soaking in the sink; sketches and paintings everywhere.

I had recently finished recording some music with a friend, and we had asked Stephen if he would like to help with the project's artwork. Earlier that day he had shown me the painting he was working on - a heavily-worked, abstract piece that depicted a treble clef amid a swirling explosion of colour and crotchets and quavers. This painting would feature on the CD itself. And now, all that was left was the album cover.

We walked down Cheadle High Street and entered the cemetery of St Mary's, a church that sits at the heart of the village. Taking advantage of their prominence above the heads of the local residents, the numbers on each of the three clock faces around the sandstone tower were replaced with 12 letters that spell out various prophecies. The clock facing south reads *FORGET NOT GOD*. Those looking from the west are urged to *TRUST THE LORD*. And, with no shortage of irony, those walking past - or entombed within - the graveyard are given the constant reminder that *TIME IS FLYING*.

I had seen that clock tower a thousand times growing up, but it was only after moving away from the area that this phrase struck me. I found the statement alone to be haunting, but a clockwork machine telling you that *time is flying*? For some reason, that had to be the front cover.

Stephen and I walked through the cemetery gates and down the old tree-lined path. Acting as impromptu art director for this final stage of the project, Stephen took a picture of the eastern clock face of St Mary's Parish Church at 4:18 pm on Saturday, March 11th, 2006.

We walked out of the churchyard, back down the high street, and parted ways at the World War II monument.

That was the last time I ever saw him.

Untitled 19 (2001)
Pen and ink

CHAPTER ONE

Seven Miles Out

ON THE CREASE between Greater Manchester and Cheshire, somewhere along that imperceptible line between the country and the city, the old River Mersey flows down from the east. Though perhaps better known, through industry and song, as the wide, yawning gateway to the Irish Sea, at this point in her journey – three miles from her source in Stockport and seven miles south of Manchester – the river cuts its way gently through open fields, wooded nature reserves, and the occasional golf course. In the summertime a grey heron wades in the shallows in silence, dragonflies catch insects above the water's surface, yellow wildflowers lean into the sun. In winter, after a snow melt or a particularly heavy spell of rain, the river swells to four, five times her normal size, creeping slowly, unstoppably, up towards the riverbank. Sometimes she overwhelms the defences completely, spilling out and flooding the fields below.

If you could carry yourself to this place in an instant and open your eyes to this landscape for the very first time, you might for a moment think you were in the English countryside. That lush green foreground. That *middle of nowhere*. But your senses would soon take over, and you would start to see the signs of the city all around: from the steel electricity pylons that cast a web around the southern panorama to the steady stream of planes making their descent to Manchester Airport, the noise from their engines merging with the dull, distant rumble of traffic from the M60 motorway.

Our story starts here, on the banks of the River Mersey, just beyond the old stone bridge on Manchester Road. This historic crossing point connects the village of Cheadle, to the south, with the much larger town of Didsbury, and by extension the City of Manchester, to the north. Pushing through the greenbelt, straight as a die, the mile-long road that links these neighbourhoods acts as a dividing line between two worlds that are at once the same and completely different. This is a *no place*, an in-between place, a road often travelled but little explored.

The Mersey springs to life at the confluence of the River Goyt and the River Tame, just outside the centre of Stockport. These two ancient waterways rise on the moors of Axe Edge and Denshaw, way up in the wilderness of the mighty Dark Peak. They join to form a river of even greater bearing – one that will travel more than 70 miles, through the country and the city, from Stockport to the Sea.

The banks are steep at the Mersey's source. But here, just a few miles downstream, where the river is joined by the Micker Brook, a sweeping meander helps to calm the water's flow. And at this meeting point of the Mersey and Ladybrook valleys, the water is easily accessible via the gentle, sandy slopes.

Evidence of human activity in and around the area dates to prehistoric times. Axe fragments that were found along the banks of the river indicate that this spot may have been an important crossing point back when the Celts roamed the land. The discovery of coins from the 4th century on the banks of the Micker Brook added weight to the theory that this shallow point was once an ancient ford.

Chad of Mercia was said to have been a frequent visitor to the area in the 7th century. A stone cross dedicated to the preacher was found not too far from the site of the Roman coins, in an area that's now known locally as the Red Rocks. With its fan-shaped arms and globular centrepiece, the Cheadle Cross remains a recognisable symbol of the village, adorning community bulletin boards and school uniforms alike.

By the year 1200, the area now known as Cheadle was still a mixture of open and wooded land. It was around this time that the first church was built in the area – an event that marked a shift away from the ancient religious site by the confluence of the Micker Brook and the Mersey to where the village sits today. The old stone cross of St Chad fell into disrepair, long forgotten until it was re-discovered hundreds of years later.

The Industrial Revolution came with the clattering of the loom, and Cheadle became an important stopping point for travellers and merchants who were heading from their factories in rural Cheshire and beyond to the great warehouse showrooms in the city centre. In 1801, the population of Cheadle was less than 1,000. Just 50 years later, at the height of the Industrial Revolution, this figure had more than tripled. This once-sleepy hamlet had been transformed into a bustling village, complete with a train station, street tram, shops, and an array of public houses and coaching inns to quench the thirst of those passing through.

As with countless villages across the length and breadth of England, Cheadle has witnessed the ever-encroaching grasp of the city. By the late 20th century, the area was home to more than 14,000 people. Much of the farmland has long been replaced by new housing estates and entertainment complexes. But despite the many changes that have taken place over the past century, this slice of suburbia has never quite lost its rural roots. The landscape is pockmarked with playing fields, open streams, hidden passageways, and thoroughfares. And for all the new housing developments and associated hustle and bustle, it's never too difficult to find solitude.

So, here we sit, somewhere along that invisible line between the country and the city. A place like any other. A place like no other. And all the while the river rolls on, weaving her way through generation after generation; their stories slip by like leaves under the bridge.

These are the stories of the children of the Mersey Valley, and this is just one of a hundred thousand tales.

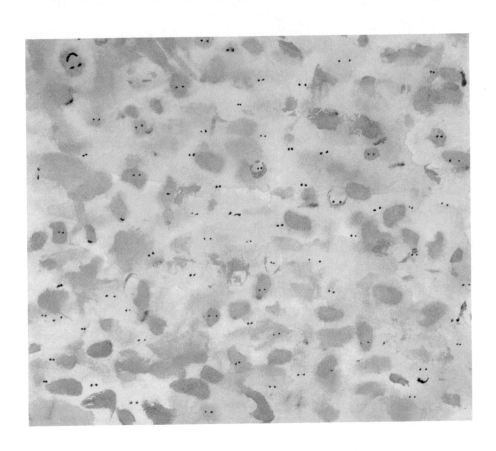

Monks (2002)
Pen and ink, watercolour

CHAPTER TWO

Once Upon a Family

STEPHEN JOSEPH WEST was born at Stepping Hill Hospital in Stockport, Greater Manchester, on February 1st, 1976. He came into the world on that crisp Sunday morning at 7:20 am. The local news headlines of the day focused on the prolonged spell of freezing weather that had swept across the UK. *Killer Cold Strikes the Old Folk / Cold Dole Workers Walk Out / Too Cold for School (Overcoat Kids Told to Stay at Home).*[2] International press wires buzzed with reports of a major art heist, as news emerged that thieves had plundered more than a hundred Picasso paintings from a palace in Avignon, France. But these events were lost on the West family; the birth of Stephen was the only news that was worthy of the day's attention. Five smiling figures gathered around the hospital bed to greet the new arrival as he adjusted to the sights and sounds of this strange new world.

Stephen's mother, Mary West, had grown up in the Cheadle Heath area of Stockport and resided in a three-bedroom house with her mother Doreen, her father Charles, and two younger sisters, Joanne and Catherine. The eldest of the siblings, Peter, had recently moved back home after studying at the University of Bradford.

The West family lived on Parkway, a pleasant, tree-lined street that links the suburban neighbourhood of the same name to Stockport Road. Around 450 homes were developed here during the interwar period, and the large front and rear gardens embody that *dig-for-victory* mentality, being both generous in proportion and wide enough to capture the sun long into the evening. Charles and Doreen were the first people to reside there, having selected the property before it was even built. Charles had served in World War II and now worked as a civil servant, while Doreen worked nights as a midwife. They were active members of the community, the smell of Charles' pipe tobacco often a precursor to a jovial "Hello!" and a chat between the young father and his neighbours as he strolled to the village shops or the local church, St Chad's.

"Dad loved his family," said Mary. "Each time he left the house, he would give everyone a kiss, without fail. And if he'd forgotten something, such as his keys, he would go around and give everyone another kiss before leaving again."

Mary was 17 when she became pregnant with Stephen, and she was 18 when he was born. The father had little involvement with his biological son. And so, during the first few months of his life, Stephen slept in a cot at the foot of Mary's bed, in a small room she shared with her two sisters.

The youngster's arrival had turned an already busy house into a hive of constant activity, but Joanne looked back on this time with fondness.

"Mary, Cath, and I shared a room that was probably the size of the smallest room in my house now," she said. "Mary had a single bed, and Cath and I had bunk beds. We had one tiny cupboard in the corner. We had one set of drawers. My dad had made us a box that fitted under our bed. We knew where everything was kept. We had an underwear draw and we each had our own drawer. When I look back, life was so simple."

"There was me, Joanne, and Cath in the back bedroom, with a cot at the end of the bed," said Mary. "Years later, I went into the house, and I walked into that back bedroom, and all the new family had in there was a cot. I couldn't see how we ever managed to fit everything in there."

This close-quarters environment no doubt contributed to the Wests forming a close bond with their young nephew and grandson. "He was everybody's child, you see," Joanne said. "Because, looking back, I know the story of Mary being pregnant. I lived the experience of her being pregnant and having Stephen. He was a beautiful baby, and he was a happy, friendly baby. People would stop in the street next to his pram and say what a beautiful baby he was."

§

At six weeks old, Stephen was christened. The occasion brought together his extended family and close family friends, many of whom were fellow church members. Among the crowd of attendees were Geoff and Irene Bird, two close friends of Charles and Doreen West. Irene and Doreen had met during their time in the *Wrens*, and their friendship continued after the war. When news spread of the soon-to-open housing estate in Cheadle Heath, the couples were able to secure homes next to one another.

"They chose adjoining drives, so it was easier to nip in and out of each other's houses," said Mary. "Auntie Irene and Uncle Geoff were like another set of parents to me and the girls."

Although Irene and Geoff were not Stephen's blood relatives, they still received the honorary titles of 'auntie' and 'uncle'.

"We all had a lovely relationship," said Geoff. "Charles and Doreen were very generous with the children. And Mary was the same with Stephen – very generous."

Geoff and Mary recalled an infant Stephen with his mousy brown hair and deep brown eyes, framed by an almost constant cheeky grin.

"From an early age he knew how to get people's attention," said Mary. "He was always shouting 'Hiya!' from his pram. And he was also meddlesome, you know. When he was two, I'd sit him in the pram outside my mum's house and he'd undo the hood of the pram. It'd be in bits. Uncle Geoff would have to come around and screw it all back together."

"He'd completely dismantle it!" said Geoff. "He used to come around to our house. If I had come home early, I would hear a little knock at the door: *knock, knock, knock*. They all became part of our family, and it was very special."

Stephen also looked back on this early period of his life with happy memories. He writes in his journal:

[We had] the best, most beautiful family in the whole wide world. Roman Catholic, not well off, but were able to get by so very, very well. Grandad and Nana, Charles and Doreen West – the most amazing, loving, intelligent grandparents. Other residents, Uncle Peter (oldest son in the family). Next, Mary Reding (my amazing mother), Auntie Jo, and the youngest, Auntie Cath. All these fantastic, loving, kind, honest, and intelligent people. It was amazing – an absolute dream to my beginning in this world. Aunty Irene and Uncle Geoff Bird lived next door, separated by little more than a garage and a hedge. The whole estate was very close-knit, and everyone was friendly. Me in the pram but loving every minute of my existence. Sat between my family. I loved my family and have the fondest memories of growing up in this community.

One of Joanne's most enduring memories of this time, in the late 1970s, was the momentous occasion of the West family's first car.

"I think I was about 11 when we got this car," she said. "It was an *Austin Cambridge*. My mother called it 'Katie'! My dad used to drive for the post office and deliver telegrams as a young person, so he had already taken his driving test. He really struggled to pass because of his eye operation, but he kept up his practising in the hope that he might have a car one day. And he was the most hilarious driver. Health and safety would have a field day today. Not long after we got this car, we all piled in to go on holiday. It was spring 1978, and Mary, Mum, Dad, Stephen, and I all stayed in a caravan. I don't know where Cath was – she might have been working. But we started off at Abersoch in Wales and then drove right down the coast to Padstow in Cornwall. Mary and I would be there in our bikinis with this cute little baby, and for us, it was more like we'd *flaunt* him. It was a way of drawing attention to ourselves. We just loved him to bits."

Prior to the birth of Stephen, Joanne noted that the two older sisters enjoyed the nightlife scene in Manchester. "When we were teenagers, we went to *Pips* and lots of other popular nightclubs," she said. "We loved dancing. Mary was wild. We were both wild! Sometimes we'd walk back in through the door just before Mum and Dad got up. I don't know how we got away with it. This was all before Stephen was born."

With the arrival of her son, Mary knew that this carefree period of her life would come to an end, but she welcomed the change with no uncertainty. And although she knew she would not be able to join her sisters on as many nights out as before, Charles and Doreen were always happy to look after their grandson, if ever she wanted to go out with her friends.

Not long after Stephen was born, Mary started a relationship with a young man named Mike Reding, who had become acquainted with the West sisters through Joanne. Stephen adored Mike, and without a doubt, the feeling was mutual.

§

A clamped-out *Austin Cambridge* was heading south along the M6 motorway. Charles was in the driver's seat, happily smoking away on his pipe. Doreen was in the passenger seat, playing with the radio. Joanne, Mary, and Stephen were in the back. Mary was crying.

"I was heading off to college in Birmingham," said Joanne.

The times were changing. Up until this point, the three sisters had shared a room together in Cheadle. And now, with Joanne heading away, this would be the first time they had been apart.

"Don't worry, I'll still come back at half-term, and you can visit any time."

Joanne's words of reassurance did little to appease Mary, as they approached the interchange.

"I'll never forget it," said Joanne. "It was my first day at college. And you know what it's like – you don't really want to draw attention to yourself. You're just about to start a whole new life. Mary was hysterical the whole journey because she didn't want me to go. I'm laughing now because I remember Stephen just lying there, sleeping."

True to their word, Mary and Mike would be frequent visitors to Joanne in Birmingham. During her time at college, Joanne met a young lady called Alweena Awan, who was from Bingley in West Yorkshire. They were flatmates for two years and became lifelong friends. Alweena would spend most of the weekends back home with her family, and Stephen would sleep in her bed with his teddy bear wrapped in his arms.

"He used to sleep in Alweena's bed," said Joanne. "It's funny to think because later on in life, they would have quite a connection."

In 1978, Mary, Mike, and Stephen moved into a two-bedroom house on Oak Grove in Cheadle. Mike was a tall, lean man with a deep voice and effortless wit. He had a marvellous way with Stephen.

"He absolutely loved Mike," said Mary. "They did a lot together. They'd go walking to the Micker Brook at Brookfield Park."

Stephen's biological father might not have been around, but Mike embraced the role with open arms. For the young boy, the feeling was mutual, as he later wrote:

Where is my dad, you might ask? Well, he had nothing to do with me.

Mike and Mary were married on September 9th. Stephen recalled the event in his journal:

> When I was two years old, my amazing mother met my soon-to-be-adoptive dad, Mike Reding. They were married not long after. Mum washed my buckle shoes in the sink whilst getting ready for the wedding. Life was great for me now. We moved into our new house, my mum, myself, and Dad. It was a small house but was more than enough room for the three of us, and it backed onto some great fields with a stream running through. Dad and myself often went for fantastic walks. We would often find ourselves suitable sticks to throw in the stream, whilst trudging through the sandbanks and other great things. In my bedroom on the walls, I had three giant Mr Men – Mr Bump (I think my favourite), Mr Strong (or was it Mr Tickle?), and finally Mr Nosey.

> Downstairs we had this beige sofa. Mother and I would often take off all the cushions and lay them all on the floor and run around the track we had made. I loved it. This was done I think when Daddy was at work. One time, I remember my mum cut her thumb on a potato peeler whilst preparing tea. I think this is my earliest memory of pain (and it wasn't even my wound). However, I felt very sad for mother.

Stephen had always been aware that Mike wasn't his biological father, but it was he whom he proudly called 'Dad'.

Their relationship would soon be cemented by law, as Mike and a newly pregnant Mary started the proceedings for Mike to formally adopt Stephen, after which he would become known as 'Stephen Joseph Reding'.

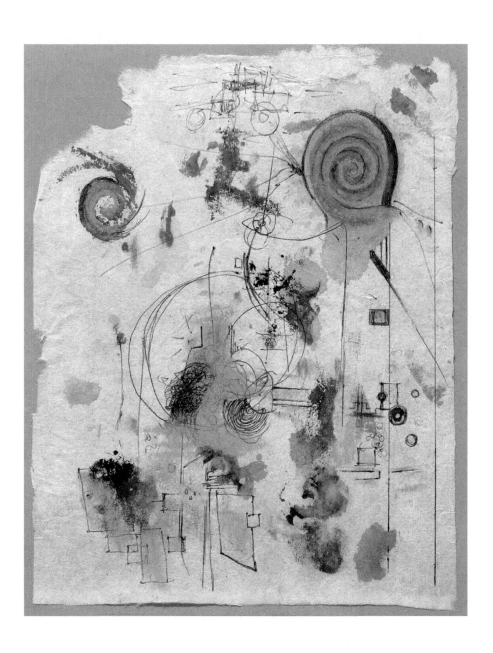

Untitled 68 (2002)
Acrylic paint, ballpoint pen

Untitled 24 (2002)
Pen and ink, watercolour

CHAPTER THREE

Northern Lights

THE REDING FAMILY welcomed baby Ruth Victoria into the world on March 19th, 1980. Stephen had recently celebrated his fourth birthday and would soon be starting his first year at primary school. Unlike many other children who find themselves in a similar situation, he exhibited little sign of jealousy upon the arrival of his sister, who was known to all by her middle name.

"He loved Victoria," said Mary. "He already had a great relationship with his dad and myself. I remember carrying him up to bed when I was pregnant with Victoria. I was lumbering up the stairs and thought, 'I'll never be able to love a child as much as I love him'. And yet, when Victoria was born – as many mums and dads realise – you don't halve your love, you just find it all again and again."

Mary added: "Although Stephen was a lovely lad, I still thought he might be very jealous of the baby, but he was brilliant with her. We did have a bit of a spell where he was very cheeky to me, and I think that was his way of saying, 'Oh, come on, there's been a change here', but overall, he was great with her. They had their ups and downs, and there were times when he thought Victoria was being good on purpose! You know, to make him look bad. He used to give her a bit of grief over that, instead of realising that she was just a good girl anyway."

Two months after the birth of Victoria, on May 21st, 1980, Stephen's adoption was finalised. He would venture out further afield on his walks with Mike. And with his sister tucked up in her cot by early evening, he was still able to enjoy some time alone with his parents.

It was during this time, as the curtains were drawn and the sun dipped over the horizon, that Stephen would be introduced to one of his lifelong passions: movies. From the big screen to rented VHS tapes, and no doubt influenced by Mike's own love of motion pictures, he would watch his favourite movies repeatedly, enraptured by the instant escapism that was on offer. He was able to recite entire scenes with astonishing accuracy, playing each character, complete with their different accents and mannerisms.

Within a year, the Redings had moved from their two-bedroom house in Cheadle to a larger property in neighbouring Cheadle Hulme. If life was previously a squeeze, the family now had space in abundance. Set on a gentle hill leading up to a small park, the three-bedroom, semi-detached property on Woods Lane had a large rear garden that backed onto a bowling green. Woods Lane High School was directly opposite, and a cluster of shops stood at the bottom of the hill. Mike was working as an automotive mechanic at a local garage. He knew the area well, having grown up in a house just on the other side of the green.

The Reding family's move to Cheadle Hulme brought them just a mile away from Mike's parents, Stephen's adoptive grandparents, Kathleen and Roy. Kath was the daughter of a shopkeeper from Cheadle Hulme, and Roy was a retired bank manager. Their manner was somewhat different to that of the carefree Wests, but Roy's conservative sensibilities would soon fade during the large family gatherings at their house – particularly after a couple of scotch and sodas when his infectious laugh would thunder through the dining room and leave the children in stitches.

"We just treated him as a grandson who had come into the family," said Kath. "We were very fond of him. We used to take him off to Blackpool for the day, that sort of thing. Mary's mum and dad were fantastic with him."

Mary's marriage to Mike brought not only two new grandparents but also an aunt in Suzanne Walker.

"I was 23 when I first met Mary and Stephen," Suzanne said. "Mary was five years younger than me, so she must have only just given birth to him when I met her for the first time. Stephen was two-and-a-half years old when they got married, and he was a lovely little boy, lovely."

§

In September 1980, taking his first steps towards independence, Stephen started his first day at the local primary school. As he grew older, escorted trips with Mary would become a kiss and a wave goodbye at the front door, as the youngster set out on the short, five-minute walk to the school, either on his own or with one of several classmates who lived nearby.

"He had a normal, happy childhood," said Mary. "He was popular in school, and on the whole, he had a great time there. He had a lovely group of friends. They all lived in the area and would often play in the park at the top of our road."

Mary recounted one story that involved Stephen during his time at primary school. "One of the teachers there was diabetic," she said. "Mr Arnold was taking assembly and he started to become poorly. He started to slur his words, and the children all thought he was being silly and making them laugh. All the children were laughing, but Stephen ran out of the assembly hall to get help. Somehow, he knew that the teacher wasn't being funny. And afterwards, the headmaster sought me out to praise Stephen's actions. He said Stephen showed such great presence of mind to run and get help when all the other kids thought the teacher was being silly and making them laugh on purpose. Stephen just thought, 'No, there's something wrong here. He's not well. This isn't right'. And he ran to get help. The teachers were all full of praise for his actions, and I was very proud of him. Mr Arnold was really on the edge of being very, very poorly."

However, almost in the same breath, Mary recounted another tale involving Stephen at primary school. This one involved a glass window being smashed on the way to school. "He was in big trouble for that," she said. "So, you know, it was swings and roundabouts."

§

The arrival of Victoria put an end to Stephen's four-year spell as an only child. It was perhaps fortunate that he got along so well with his sister, as the Reding family would soon start to expand further. In 1982, when Stephen was six and Victoria was two, the youngsters were joined by a new baby brother, Andrew, followed by Christopher a year later.

Reflecting on the growth of the family during this time, Mary joked that there was now "little time for laughter", but in truth, she made it her priority to raise and nurture the four children in a warm, loving household, just like the one that Joanne, Cath, and herself had enjoyed. Mary was successful in her endeavours, but there was one thing a house of this size could rarely be: quiet. But this suited Stephen just fine. He had enjoyed a front-row seat in the West household when growing up and was well-prepared for the ups and downs of life on Woods Lane.

Joanne draws a parallel between the busy, crowded family life that Stephen was introduced to when he was born and that of the Reding household in Cheadle Hulme. "It was a crazy, crazy lifestyle," she said. "Stephen's home life was a continuation of his life on Parkway because there was never a quiet time. There was always this bombardment of people arriving, people going, situations happening, and relationships exploding. There was no sort of… steady. It was unpredictable. So, he had to be very robust in the way that he dealt with it. And he was. He was very open-minded."

Stephen embraced his role as the oldest sibling, particularly as he now had a readymade, captive audience and a constant source of amusement on tap. At the best of times, he led the charge, with his siblings absorbing his every word like sponges. He was the ringleader, holding court with the youngsters and making them laugh with his endless stream of impressions and comical facial expressions.

Stephen quickly learned that his siblings would make the ideal test subjects for his various experiments. His brother Andrew was often first in line – willingly or not.

"At the back of the old house, there used to be a bowling green," said Andrew. "But at the top of Woods Lane, past Thorn Grove, there is a park. Me and Ste were on the seesaw. It was one of those old-fashioned seesaws made from iron. Ste said, 'Okay, any minute now I'm going to jump off'. I remember thinking, 'I don't like the sound of this', but before I could do anything he jumped off and I went flying. I fell off and cut my head!"

Andrew added: "I remember Ste, even from a young age, always going on about taekwondo and karate. I must have been about four. And in the middle of the night, Ste was like, 'Right, Andy, I've got a new karate move'. I think *The Karate Kid* had recently come out, and Ste used to always wear this white bandana, like Danny LeRusso. He told me to crouch down because he wanted to hit my face softly, just to show me the move and what he would do if he was ever in the situation that I – a four-year-old child – was now in. Ste crouched down and got ready to demonstrate the 'soft' force kick. But he hit me full on, and my two milk teeth folded into the roof of my mouth. There was a lot of screaming. Dad rushed in. I felt sorry for Ste because I knew that he didn't do it on purpose. I thought he was really going to get into trouble for it."

"He was ever so good with the children," his Nana Kath remembered, fondly.

"He shot me in the head once!" said Victoria. "Dad used to have these rifle guns, the pellet ones, and he had an air pistol, too. Ste got his hands on the air pistol. It was a proper metal one. It had a thing that you pushed down into the barrel, and it shot out. He obviously didn't know the barrel section shot out when you pressed the trigger. He held it up against my head and pulled the trigger! I think it knocked me out. All I can remember was coming around, and I was up against the wall at the side of the house. Grandad was babysitting, and Stephen was like, 'Don't you dare tell Grandad, don't you dare!' I had blood streaming down my face! He followed me around for a few hours to make sure I didn't tell anyone. I have a little scar under my hair, it's like a tiny little indent. But I genuinely don't think he knew it shot out because he held it at close range. It's like Andy's teeth – it's just one of those things that happen when you're a kid. Years later, completely out of the blue, he actually sent me a message to apologise for doing it."

Aside from losing his front teeth a few years too early, Andrew wouldn't have changed a thing. "I loved Ste," he said. "We were good mates. Yes, I was the fall guy, the crash test dummy. I loved it though because it was my way of doing stuff with Ste."

§

The move to Woods Lane marked the start of a new chapter for the Redings. It was a time of optimism and growth. However, in 1984 this balance was interrupted when the family was rocked by the death of Mary's mother, Doreen.

"She was only 59 when she died," said Kath. "She knew she was ill, but didn't want the news to spoil Mary, Mike, and the children's first family holiday. Mary knew something wasn't right. She said, 'Mum, tell me what's wrong with you'. Doreen said to Mary, 'You go and get your holiday, and we'll talk about it when you get back'."

The news came as a blow to both the West and the Reding families, and it had a lasting impact on Stephen.

"Charlie was never short of company," said Kath, who was there to witness the family coming together in the wake of the tragedy. "Peter had moved home due to health reasons, and Charlie always used to visit Mary. He used to help look after the kids and would read to them."

If there were any silver lining to this situation, Doreen's passing would result in Charles spending even more time with the Redings. He would often appear seemingly out of nowhere as the kids were playing outside, his face emerging from the side door, as he greeted each of his grandchildren with a warm hug.

§

David Reding was born in November 1985, bringing the number of boys in the family to four. Stephen's extended family would also grow to include several new members. His Aunt Joanne now resided in a house on the banks of the River Tay in Perth, Scotland, after having met her future husband while she was teaching in London. With the married name of Workman, she had three children, Harry, Jack, and Sophie. Mary's youngest sister, Catherine, lived in Stourbridge with her husband Chris and their two children, Emma and Simon. On Stephen's adoptive side of the family, Mike's younger sister Suzanne Walker lived in Cheadle with her husband and children, James and Lauren.

With a total of 18 youngsters in one generation, and still more to come, family gatherings were lively affairs. Shaky home video footage of the time reveals a typical weekend scene in a park, with the kids playing cricket and throwing the frisbee, and the adults sitting in a circle on the grass and laughing. On occasion, the Reding and Walker children would spend their Saturdays at their grandparents Kath and Roy's house in Cheadle Hulme. Their house backed onto some playing fields that led to a bridge over the Micker Brook. These family visits would turn into day-long affairs, culminating in three generations fumbling through a ramshackle game of rounders or playing around barefoot in the brook. Of course, Stephen was often at the centre of attention, whipping the children up into a hyperactive frenzy with his endless jokes and antics.

Stephen's cheeky nature sometimes grated on Roy. Perhaps, as the oldest child, he felt it was his responsibility to test the limit of his grandfather's boundaries, but test him he did, and through various means. This would include sneaking upstairs to Roy's electric organ and blasting on the keys with all the passion of a seasoned jazz musician. The cacophony of noise would, unsurprisingly, send his grandfather screaming up the stairs after him.

In addition to summer holidays in Wales, the Redings would be frequent visitors to Perth, where Joanne now lived with her family. Stephen started a tradition among the Reding children of travelling to Scotland, either to study or simply for a vacation. The Workman family had a holiday home in the foothills of the Cairngorms. This was a place full of mystery and unfamiliarity that Stephen was keen to maximise on, as he thought of new ways to scare his sister.

"I think I was about seven," said Victoria. "Auntie Joanne took me and Stephen on holiday. They had a cottage in Scotland near the *Glenlivet* distillery, and we'd been there before with Mum. The cottage had been left to them by a family member. I remember the place so well. If I went there now, I would probably know where to go. This place had about five houses and a post office. And there was a road with a few houses, the tiniest church you've ever seen, and a whisky distillery. It was in the middle of nowhere. This time, we'd gone with just Auntie Joanne. I was seven or eight, Stephen was 11 or 12, and we'd gone for a little walk down the road. There was this derelict cottage, and Stephen said, 'You stay here, I'll go and check it out'. So, he went in. I just stood there on the road and the next thing I heard was, 'Quick! Get him! I've got the rope; you tie him up!' I just remember screaming and running back up the road to go and get help. But Stephen had staged the whole thing by putting on these different voices. He must have realised he scared me a bit too much because he came running after me, grabbed hold of me and, like the pellet gun incident, said, 'Don't you dare tell anyone!' And I didn't. I think the first time I told that story to anyone else was when I was 16 or 17. I never told a soul!"

§

Stephen started secondary school in 1987. His journey to primary school took less than five minutes, but the commute to Woods Lane High School was even shorter, as it was located directly opposite the Reding house.

Stephen had many friends during his school years, but he would become lifelong pals with three young men. Although Ian Harding wasn't in the same school year as Stephen, the pair became fast friends when he moved to the area.

"I moved to Manchester when I was about eight years old," said Ian. "I grew up in Leeds and then we moved to Cheadle Hulme. Ste was living on Woods Lane, near the school, and both of our houses backed onto the park with the bowling green. I first met him in that park. I was in the year above him, but we always used to hang out."

The pair became close friends with two other lads, Matt Fletcher and Jamie Hirst, who were in the same school year as Stephen. The four pals soon became inseparable, united by their love of music, movies, and skateboarding.

"He had a lovely group of friends in secondary school," said Mary, who noted that it was around this time that Stephen started to take great interest in his appearance. "When he was 11, he saved up some money and bought himself this huge pair of sunglasses. 'Shades', he called them. This was the first time he'd had a big say in what he was wearing. He had this yellow stripy shirt and a pair of white trousers, and he was walking around with these shades on. And he turned to me and said, 'Mum, do you think I look like a cool dude?' It was the first time I'd ever heard the phrase. I said, 'Well, *you* think you do!' And again, we set off laughing. Stephen and I could dissolve into laughter with just one look at each other. We wouldn't even know what we were laughing at half the time. This stemmed from the times we had when he was a little toddler. I had lots of fun with Stephen, and I think that took us into our adult lives."

Stephen's fashion sense wasn't lost on his siblings back then in the neon-tinged 80s. "I don't know if Mum's talking about the same yellow shirt he used to have," said Victoria. "It was this yellow shirt with people on. It was far too big for him. He used to wear it with these pink shorts and his *Reebok Pump* trainers."

"He was very good-looking," said Mary. "And if he had one fault, he could be a bit vain. There wasn't a lot of money floating around, and he was aware that he had to wait until Christmas and birthdays for things. He liked nice things but was happy to wait. For example, he wouldn't want any old shoes for school – not when there were branded *Kickers* and things to buy."

Stephen had a keen eye for fashion that would follow him through to his adult life. Glancing through old family photographs shows Stephen sporting a range of styles throughout his teenage years, from mod-style button-down shirts and jeans to out-there bubble jackets and sportswear. He was always replete with the latest brands and items bought with money earned through household chores or delivering papers and leaflets.

Incidentally, Stephen's famed *Reebok Pump* trainers were not chosen purely for fashion reasons. During his time at secondary school, he started to take an active interest in basketball. A regulation-height net was set up in the back garden, where Stephen would practice his three-pointers or attempt to slam dunk the ball, despite it being far too high for him.

In addition to basketball, Stephen took a keen interest in athletics, and this led to him becoming sports captain when he was 13. He also had a penchant for the stage, as a theatre programme for the church performance of *Snow White and the Seven Dwarfs* in January 1991 listed Mike, Mary, and Stephen at the top of the bill as The King, The Queen, and The Prince. The following year Stephen played Pip Appleblossom in *Beauty and the Beast*.

These extracurricular activities became an important part of Stephen's life, but when it came to his academic performance, things didn't get off to the smoothest of starts.

"Overall, he did well at secondary school," said Mary, "But he was never academically brilliant. He needed to work for the grades and would be okay – unless he stopped working. And when he was underachieving, we would get letters. He once hid a letter from me regarding three subjects he was underachieving in. I got a phone call from the teacher and it all came out, the fact that he'd hidden this letter. And he was in big trouble over that. But then he just seemed to get on with school life. He had friends, played his basketball, he was into fashion."

Victoria recalls her eldest brother taking a *laissez-faire* approach to his education. "Mum once said to me, 'Oh, Stephen works so hard. He comes in from school, he goes straight upstairs, and gets his books out'. Then she said, 'Victoria, go and tell Stephen it's dinner time'. I went into his room, and he was fast asleep!"

Snoozing through his homework wasn't the only bad habit Stephen picked up during this time at school.

"He started smoking at a young age," said Andrew. "I remember he picked me up from primary school once. We were walking home, and some girls came over to me and said, 'Do you know your brother smokes?' Ste said I could tell Mum if I wanted, but I didn't."

Stephen's education wasn't always plain sailing, but one subject that he enjoyed throughout his time at school was art. Indeed, this would go on to become one of his life's biggest passions.

"He was always drawing and doodling, from an early age," said Mary, who recalled how his younger siblings would often try to copy his cartoon creations.

"Stephen did a beautiful chalk drawing for his Grandad West," said Joanne. "That's when I first noticed his talent. It was his hand inside his grandad's hand. It was a Christmas present for him when he was in secondary school."

§

As the years went by, some distance started to grow between Stephen and his siblings. It was perhaps natural that the 14-year-old would want to spend less time with his younger family members. Those close to him noted that Stephen was in somewhat of an awkward place during these years: too young to sit with the grownups as they sipped their *digestifs*, but too old to be hanging around with the primary school kids and watching cartoons on TV. Overall, this wasn't a huge problem: Stephen had a close group of peers with whom he would spend an increasing amount of time. And during family gatherings, he was more than happy to keep himself occupied by listening to his *Walkman* and doodling at the top of the stairs.

Finding solitude sometimes proved easier said than done, as he endured a constant stream of questions and attention-grabbing antics from his siblings and cousins. For them, Stephen was a repository of information. He was full of anecdotes and entertainment and had developed a penchant for spinning tall tales. He was a conduit for the ghost stories and urban myths that filtered down through the playground. At his best, Stephen would take centre stage and hold his young audience captive with his stories. Just his entering a room could leave the children buckled over, as he would casually lean himself up against the wall to say,

"Guys, guys – I don't feel too good…"

And with his fist at the ready, hidden beneath his sweatshirt and his empty sleeve tucked into his trouser pocket, he would punch out an epic *Alien*-style

Chestburster, complete with twisted expressions of horror and groans. Even a simple game of darts couldn't be played the standard way, as he would proceed to shun all rules and regulations by facing directly away from the board and spinning himself around with a crazed look on his face and no chance to aim before launching the dart as hard as he could.

The eldest of the Reding siblings had fallen in love with movies at a young age. He absorbed popular culture like a sponge, and now, as a teenager armed with a membership card to the local video shop, he was able to take his passion to a new level. The genres of choice? Action, horror, and comedy.

"He used to ask me to list my top 10 films and then argue if my films didn't match his favourites," said Mary.

As a lightning rod for all things 'cool', Stephen provided a constant supply of new movies for his younger family members. On the downside, they soon realised that the number '18' on the VHS box was there for a reason.

"James and I watched *Predator* at the age of 10," Andrew recalled. "Ste was babysitting when I was staying at Auntie's. The movie choice was *RoboCop* or *Predator*."

"I think it was a rite of passage," added David. "He made me watch *Total Recall* at the age of nine. He tried to tell me that all women in the future would have three breasts."

Stephen delighted in scaring the younger ones, but they also enjoyed being allowed to rehearse their emotions in his company.

"He had a brilliant, wicked sense of humour," said Joanne.

"Oh, he was a bit of a blagger!" said Mary. "But they all loved his stories."

Life wasn't without its arguments. As well as having the innate ability to make his brothers and sister laugh, he also knew how to upset them. The term 'bully' might not be too strong a word, as Stephen would use his age, physical stature, and mental dexterity to his advantage – at times reducing his sibling to tears with a vicious comment or submission move.

Although there were many occasions when Stephen would assert his authority over his siblings, more often than not he was laughing with them, not at them. And for all the times that ended in tears, there were a hundred occasions that saw them all laughing.

"Despite the day-to-day squabbles, Stephen liked to be a protective older brother, very much so," said Mary. "This applied to all his extended family, really. He very much took his role as the eldest quite seriously."

§

By 1989, the once-spacious house on Woods Lane was becoming too small. And with another baby on the way, it was time for the Redings to move again. This proved to be a welcome change, as they purchased a four-bedroom, semi-detached property on the Parkway estate where Mary had grown up and where her father still lived.

Although the location of the new house on Lighthorne Road now required Stephen to take a bus to school, for the first time since he was six, he had his own bedroom. And he loved it.

Stephen wrote:

It was time to move to a new house again. We were running out of room. We moved back to the same estate that I was born into, just around the corner. It was lovely to be so near to all our close family again. Uncle Peter was living at my very first house, along with Gentle Grandad Charlie. Auntie Irene and Uncle Geoff were still next door to them, just around the corner. Through all the years leading up to now, we had spent so many weekends there and so many special trips, days out, and events that, really, we had never been away.

I had my own room – the first in many years. John Francis was born, and it was pretty great for us. We definitely had one of the biggest families when I was at school, that was for certain, but it was quite wonderful. We always got by. I went to Woods Lane, which was ideal because that was the road that we lived on. I was always a good student and on the whole pretty good at school. Perhaps I would sometimes act like a clown (showing off, I think) but no major trouble. I should have tried harder because I love knowledge these days.

"He had a perfectly normal life," said Mary. "He was what I would call an 'average kid' – he did his work, he didn't do his work; he got in trouble, was good as gold; he got on with his sister and brothers, and he would squabble with them."

Going to the Party (2006)
Oil paint on canvas

CHAPTER FOUR

Hit

ON WEDNESDAY, NOVEMBER 6th, 1991, at the age of 15, Stephen Reding boarded a bus from Woods Lane School in Cheadle Hulme to the neighbouring town of Cheadle Heath – a 20-minute journey he took every weekday on his way home. He was in his final year of secondary school and in preparation for his GCSE exams.

On this day, which was, by all accounts, a day like any other day, Stephen was accompanied by Nick Shaw, a friend of his younger brother, Andrew, who lived across the street from the Reding family.

Stephen and Nick disembarked the bus at Bird Hall Lane and set out on the short walk home when they were spotted by a group of five older males. The youths, estimated to be around 18 years old, motioned as though they were about to cross the road, but instead turned and started to walk towards the pair of schoolboys.

Nick, who was four years younger than Stephen, assumed they were his friends and continued to walk on as they approached. He turned the corner. Stephen was soon surrounded.

"What are you looking at?" said one of the lads.

"Nothing. I'm not looking at you."

Time slowed to a standstill.

Fade to black.

Ko Tao (2000)
Pen and ink, watercolour

CHAPTER FIVE

Picking up the Pieces

THE STREETS WERE empty. The road was silent. Stephen was laid out on the cold concrete. Any sign of the lads who assaulted him had vanished without a trace. But time caught up with itself, and almost immediately after the attack, Stephen was spotted by an elderly couple who were driving by, just beyond the traffic lights at the junction of Bird Hall Lane and Edgeley Road. They pulled over and hurried out of the car.

Stephen responded to their voices with a groan. As he slowly regained consciousness, the passers-by managed to help him into the back seat of their car. After asking him several times what had happened and where he lived, Stephen was able to string enough words together to direct them to his house.

§

Mary saw the car pull up from the living room window. She came to the door and ran towards her son when she saw him stumbling down the path.

"Stephen! What's happened?"

"Mum, I've been hit. I don't remember anything else now until I got home, and I'm piecing this together." He motioned to the couple in the car. "They've brought me home. I've got to get in."

Stephen did eventually piece the incident together. Years later, he committed his account of the assault to paper, as he wrote in his journal:

I was doing my first GCSEs (final year of high school). Whilst walking home from school – not long after I had got off the bus – I was approached by five older lads, who I would call *scallies*. They were not from around here. I had never seen any of them before. I knew the group of five meant for trouble, as they circled me and started pushing me (I was worried). That soon disappeared as one of them, from the corner of my eye, uppercut me to the jaw. I was out cold – sparked on the street.

A car pulled over. I somehow guided them to where I lived. (How I managed to do that, to this day, I don't know.) I was totally out of it. Totally dazed. Concussed. The nice couple said they had seen a group of lads running away before they had pulled over to help me. I think they must have gotten scared after I was sparked out.

"I don't know how I even told them where I lived," Stephen said to Mary, as she assessed his injuries.

"He said there were a few of them and that they were older than him," his mother recounted. "*I don't know how I got back*, he said. *I was just talking to Nick. The next thing, Nick says 'see ya' and there they were.* They must have whacked him so hard, because they cracked his jaw, broke his teeth."

The motive behind the attack on Stephen, in broad daylight on that Wednesday afternoon, will perhaps never be known, but he maintained that the assault was unprovoked.

"They said, 'What are you looking at?' But I wasn't looking at them funny," he told Mary. "I just said, 'I'm not looking at you'. I wasn't stupid, Mum."

In Stephen's written account of the event, he implies that the gang may have been looking to steal his clothing. ("I remember I was wearing my new *Naff* coat and *Reebok Pump* basketball trainers," he writes.) Although it's unclear whether his branded attire made him a target, the fashion-conscious youngster was glad to hold onto his possessions, as the youths ran away after punching him without warning:

At least I got to keep my new threads and treads, which had been acquired through a number of hard weekends' work gardening for Mum. The downside of it was the fact that I had a broken jaw and several bruises on my head.

Perhaps the group of lads were looking to steal Stephen's belongings, or maybe they were just out for trouble on that fateful day. Either way, the assailants were quick to flee. They were never identified by the police and never seen again.

It wasn't only the gang of five who vanished without a trace; the couple who found Stephen and helped him – truly his Good Samaritans that day – were never again seen by Stephen or the Reding family.

"I sort of waved a thank you, and they waved from inside the car and drove off," Mary said. "We never saw that couple again, and that's one regret I have. But we are so glad they did what they did. They were very kind. I just waved to them, and off they went."

In the immediate aftermath of the incident, Stephen was taken to the hospital, where he was bandaged up and had his jaw x-rayed. His jaw was wired shut to help it heal with correct alignment, and he would later have two minor operations to help fix it back in place.

"He had to have hospital treatment because he had a cracked jaw and some broken teeth," said Mary.

Following the medical treatment, the police visited the Reding household and took a statement from Stephen. He was also interviewed by a victim support officer. On both occasions, with his jaw aching, he reluctantly recounted his hazy story.

"It was bad," said his brother, Andrew. "It was really bad. They knocked him out cold. He must have hit his head on the ground without his hands to break his fall."

Despite the seriousness of the attack, Stephen remained calm throughout the ordeal. News of the assault quickly spread to his family and friends, many of whom came to visit him when he was, on the doctor's recommendations, confined to his bed. However, after the initial trauma, he expressed a desire to move on from the incident and continue to study for his upcoming GCSE exams.

Victoria recalls one brief incident from the early days of Stephen's recovery that suggests her brother was quick to return to his usual ways: "His jaw was wired, and he half whispered, half groaned, 'Mum, can I have some ice cream? It's the only thing I can eat'. Mum said he better not, but he eventually persuaded her. She walked out of the room to get the ice cream, and he gave me a smile. I can't say he milked the situation because it was serious and he was in a lot of pain, but he still had that glint in his eye."

§

Exactly one week after the assault on Bird Hall Lane, Stephen had his first seizure.

§

"I'll never forget it," said Mary. "One of our close family friends had epilepsy and I had often been with them when they had a seizure, so I knew what an epileptic seizure was. Our friend happened to be here with us that day. I could hear some commotion and walked into the living room. And I knew straight away because I had seen my friend have a *grand mal*. And I was looking at Stephen on the floor in the kitchen. I'll never forget it. It was like we were all in a play, but the actors were playing the wrong roles. And I looked across to my friend, and he knew straight away what was happening, and I ran over to Stephen, and I kept thinking, 'The wrong person's doing this, it shouldn't be you that's doing this, why are you doing this?' And I was trying to help him. He still had his injuries – his jaw was still wired. We went to the doctor and then to the hospital."

An estimated 600,000 individuals – around one in every 100 people – have epilepsy in the UK.[3] Many people are born with it, and everyone has the potential to develop or acquire the condition, particularly following external physical trauma – a so-called traumatic brain injury (TBI).

According to the *Epilepsy Foundation of America*, motor vehicle accidents, firearms, falls, sports, and physical violence are the leading causes of TBIs that result in post-traumatic epilepsy:

> TBI is the most significant cause of symptomatic epilepsy in people from 15 to 24 years of age. Post-traumatic epilepsy (PTE) is by definition from a focal (localised) injury, and the frontal and temporal lobes are the most frequently affected regions. The likelihood of developing (post-traumatic) epilepsy after a TBI is higher with greater severity of the trauma. Generally, seizures after TBI can appear early (within one week of the injury) or later.[4]

Epilepsy is sometimes viewed as a mysterious affliction, and perhaps this is due to its abstract definition: It is simply classed as a medical condition where brain activity becomes abnormal, resulting in seizures or periods of unusual behaviour, sensations, and sometimes loss of awareness.

"When people have epilepsy, you get these sort of electrical storms occurring in parts of the brain," said Professor Matthew Walker, head of clinical and experimental epilepsy at University College London's Queen Square Institute of Neurology. "Usually this arises from one specific part of the brain – especially after a traumatic brain injury. We divide the seizures up into what we term 'generalised seizures' that happen suddenly throughout the whole brain. These are often genetically determined. And then there are 'focal seizures', which are seizures that arise in one part of the brain, and then they can spread through the brain. If they just stay in one part of the brain, the electrical storm can cause whatever that part of the brain does. So, if it's in the temporal lobe, for example, which is to do with memory, then people will often get things like intense feelings of déjà vu, hallucinations of past memories, and intense feelings like that. And then if the storm spreads throughout the whole brain, you get the tonic-clonic seizure, which is the sort of maximal seizure that most people will recognise."

Professor Walker [no relation to the author] underlined the many ways in which epilepsy can impact an individual's life.

"Depending on where in the brain the seizures are occurring, or the part of the brain that is damaged, it can have a profound effect upon behaviour, mood, and cognition," he said. "Epilepsy is more than just seizures, it's many other things."

For Stephen, in addition to the trauma and confusion that was brought about by his seizures, his condition required seemingly endless tiresome trips to doctors, specialists, hospitals, and medical suites, complete with electroencephalography (EEG) scans, various medication, and the unwelcome realisation that he would never be able to drive. Still, years after the fact, Stephen described this time in his life with remarkable light-heartedness:

Seven days later I suffered from an epileptic fit (*grand mal* seizure – this is where you will violently shake and eventually knock yourself out). Whoops!

§

The Reding family friend who was there to witness Stephen's first seizure was a welcome presence, particularly as it became clear that he would have to live with epilepsy for the rest of his life. "They don't treat you for epilepsy until you've had three *grand mal* seizures," Mary explained. "But Stephen's was different, and of course, he did eventually have more than three."

Stephen put on a brave face as the seriousness of his condition settled in, but although he didn't often show it, the onset of his epilepsy had come as a big shock. It had thrown him into a state of inner turmoil and would continue to have a profound effect on his life for many years to come.

The gravity of the situation was not lost on his brother John, who was just two years old at the time. "It's pretty much the first concrete, real thing that I can remember from when I was young," he said.

"I didn't realise the severity of it all until he started having seizures," added his brother, Chris. "And then it was tough because every two or three months he would have a really bad seizure. The first one I saw was the toughest because I remember thinking, 'It shouldn't be like this'. They were horrible. He didn't deserve what happened to him, but as far as I knew, growing up, he was never resentful."

Stephen took his GCSE exams in June 1992, and despite the ordeal, he managed to pass them all. Summer had returned, and the kids played in the cul-de-sacs and in the parks and in the fields nearby. The chaos would subside when they were treated to ice cream from a van passing by; a moment of calm before the escapades resumed, out there on the avenues and on the freshly cut grass.

Stephen would continue to join in on those fun-filled summer days – back at the centre of attention, spinning the children around by their hands and feet, and causing them to double over in fits of laughter with nothing but the flick of an eyebrow. But although their screams of delight offered a temporary diversion, it would be many years until he could block out the distant sound of the footsteps that tipped and tapped and echoed away – away, away, down Bird Hall Lane.

Self-portrait in a Vase (2006)
Chalk pastel, charcoal pencil

Self-portrait in a Sketchbook (2006)
Chalk pastel, charcoal pencil

CHAPTER SIX

A Portrait of the Young Man as an Artist

AFTER FINISHING HIGH SCHOOL in the summer of 1992, Stephen started to consider his future options. Many of his friends were taking an extended break before they continued their studies in September. Others picked a trade and stepped onto the first rung of the ladder. Both of these options were open to Stephen, but in all truth, he didn't know what to do.

Following the police interviews and the victim support meetings, a case file was handed to the UK Criminal Injuries Compensation Board. In light of his newfound neurological condition and the numerous operations that had been carried out on his jaw, Stephen was informed that he would receive compensation for his injuries. The amount, which would be awarded by the state once he turned 18, came to just over £10,000. ("Yippee, give me more epilepsy," Stephen wrote, describing his initial reaction to the news.) He was understandably excited, but his anticipation of the money – a huge amount for any teenager – was offset by the fact that he would need to take medication on a daily basis, would be unable to drive, and would likely live under the shadow of the term 'tonic-clonic seizure' for the rest of his life. This sense of uncertainty was only heightened when Mary and Mike announced that they were separating.

Stephen disliked the hospital visits, the tests, and the endless examinations, but he was surrounded by words of encouragement from those around him. At one point, Stephen's medication appeared to be having adverse side effects, and Mary asked the doctor to re-evaluate his prescription.

"Stephen said he used to feel 'doped up' – those were his words – and would skip taking his medication to feel more with it," Mary said. "This led to a new set of problems because his body and mind had to cope with this inconsistency."

As he waited for the compensation money to come through, Stephen decided to look for a job. The young man knew that some doors were now closed to him because of his epilepsy. He had, at one point, expressed the idea of wanting to become a fireman. It's not known whether this was a serious desire or a fleeting teenage dream, but either way, this career path was no longer an option for him. Nevertheless, after some searching, Stephen's first full-time job came in the form of a plumbing apprenticeship for a company based in Burnage. Each morning he would cycle from Cheadle Heath to Cheadle, up Manchester Road and across the bridge over the River Mersey, before a final mile ride up Kingsway. He would be at the van by eight o'clock in the morning, and on some evenings, he wouldn't get home until seven or eight o'clock at night. The hours were long, and the money wasn't great, but the apprenticeship promised a decent future wage, and Stephen seemed to take to the job well. Despite these outward appearances, however, something wasn't quite right inside his mind:

> After school finished, I actually did a plumbing and building apprenticeship. Ha! I think I was mostly trying to prove to myself that I was 'normal', just like anybody else. That my newfound illness would not deter me. A job seemed like probably the hardest challenge at the time. I stuck at it for two years on thirty-odd quid a week – what was I thinking?

Stephen pushed on with the apprenticeship. The long hours resulted in him having little free time during the week, and so Saturdays were intermittently reserved for hospital visits – journeys he was quickly growing to despise. These trips were necessary, however; in addition to the impact on his mental health, the trauma of his recurring seizures would often result in Stephen dislocating his shoulder. This left him with a near-constant dull ache that required regular medical attention. His condition started to weigh heavy on his heart:

> What also went on as I grew through my teens was this fucking epilepsy. SEIZURES. DISLOCATION OF JOINTS. EEGs. BRAIN SCANS. Pods stuck all over me to monitor my heart. I started to really dislike hospitals. I was sports captain all through school and played basketball for several teams. 100

metres – 13 secs. Would run 10 miles. I most certainly would have been driving as soon as I was old enough. Instead, I was a guinea pig – put on an extremely high dose of anti-epileptic drugs. Why the fuck do I have to deal with this? It wasn't me who caused this. I wasn't born with it and it all happened for... er... why?

Looking back, it would have been no surprise to learn that Stephen was suffering from some degree of post-traumatic stress. But this wasn't something he was quick to divulge to those around him – and neither was the fact that two young lads at the plumbing business had started to bully him over his condition.

§

Stephen remained a popular young man throughout his late teens. His chiselled features and sharp clothes were now augmented by a thin silver neck chain and an equally thin line shaved into his left eyebrow. His good looks didn't escape the attention of the females in his group, and – true to the aim he expressed to his mother, back then when he was just a kid in shades – he was indeed regarded as something of a "cool dude" among his peers.

Mixing in various social circles, it wasn't long before Stephen was introduced to alcohol, and later soft drugs. As is the case with many teenagers below the legal drinking age, Stephen and his friends would sneak alcohol out of their parent's houses, try their luck getting served in the students' union or some local dive, or quietly plead with passers-by outside the off-licence to do them a favour, tenner in hand and the prospect of a night being made or broken reflected in their eyes. Although he had smoked cigarettes from a young age, and by this point was smoking openly in front of his parents, it's not known exactly when Stephen first felt the haze of a dark, sticky resin that had been added to the rolling paper. But once he did, he embraced the feeling with open arms:

From the time of the assault and into my second year of plumbing, I used to go out with all my friends, and they would be all experimenting with cannabis.

Not me, though. This was completely out of the question. Not when I now have such a problem: EPILEPSY. (I hated it. Inside it drove me to tears – but I put on a front. I was 'normal' like everybody else.) This went on for some years – where I would watch my friends experiment, go wild, and have fun. My mum and family would say how strong I was – how well I was dealing with it all. But something was gnawing at me inside. I hated having this. I would rebel. I *would* take drugs like I had seen so many of my friends do through the years.

Perhaps alcohol and cannabis offered some sort of escape. Whatever the reason, once Stephen took the decision to partake, drugs would play a role in his life for many years to come. A doorway had been opened in his mind, and he certainly didn't want to miss out on the party. The young explorer was by no means alone in his recreational drug taking. He was no different from the tens of thousands of other young (and fully grown) adults who dabbled in chemical substances other than alcohol, such as cannabis, amphetamines, LSD, cocaine, and ecstasy.

Stephen, Ian, Matt, and Jamie's friendship grew throughout secondary school and into their young adulthood. Around this time, two other lads joined the group: Josh Brunswick and Russ Henderson. The six were brought together by their shared taste in music, along with a proclivity for art and experimentation.

"I did my A-Levels at Woods Lane," said Ian, "but then I went to college to study art. And it was there that I met Josh, who was on my art course, and he became a good friend of ours. And Josh, Ste, Matt, Jamie, and I all used to hang out together. We had another mate, Russ, whose parents had a huge house in Handforth. The house had a separate garage, and in the garage was a pool table with sofas and other furniture. So, we used to go and play pool and smoke weed. Even when Russ was away, me and Ste used to go on our own. We would play chess and just get absolutely caned."

Sharing his thoughts on Stephen during this time, Ian said: "He was so hilarious – he would wind people up. I've got a good mate, Sean. He and Ste never really saw eye to eye. Sean was a big Manchester United fan, and Ste would always make fun of their goalkeeper, you know, and just wind him up. But then, there was one night, I think I had gone home, and for some reason they ended up together, just the two of them getting wasted. And they spent the whole evening together, and they just clicked. Sean always speaks fondly of him now."

Stephen would, inevitably, watch his friends take their driving lessons and eventually pass their tests. But he reacted positively to the situation by purchasing a new mountain bike. And from that moment forward, Stephen would always be in possession of a stylish form of two-wheeled transportation.

When he wasn't hanging out at the garage den with his friends in Handforth, he was most likely to be found in his room, listening to music, playing games on the *Amiga*, or doodling away. Art was fast becoming a serious hobby for Stephen – and the results showed. The young artist was filling sketchpads and random pieces of paper with anything that came into his head: far-out characters and caricature gangsters, subway-style graffiti text, alien invasions, and bizarre dystopian landscapes with dozens of stick figures falling from the sky to meet their doom on the spikes below. The subject matter may have been a little crude, but he certainly had talent.

§

Rebecca "Becky" Reding was born in November 1992. ("Now our number seven," Stephen writes.) Although his sister was a welcome addition to the family, as a teenager entering young adulthood, Stephen generally had little time for his siblings' games. The distance was growing wider – the four-to-seventeen-year gap between himself and his brothers and sisters now appeared as a chasm to adolescent eyes.

"When I was younger, with Stephen it was strange," Chris explained. "We didn't really know him back then because he was just so popular with his friends. He had a good group of friends who were always coming and going. He was a lot older than most of us. It's not that he didn't have the time of day for us, but when his mates came around, you could just tell he didn't want to be bothered. He would always say, 'What are you doing here? Go away'. Because we were all young, we saw these older teenagers and we were curious, starry-eyed."

Andrew added: "When we moved to Cheadle Heath, we did gain a bit of distance in Ste. I mean, how many rooms were there in the old house? Three? In the old house, we *had* to be close because we were living in each other's pockets."

In the same stroke, however, Andrew recalls how Stephen, now earning a weekly wage, would occasionally venture downstairs to ask one of his brothers to go to the shop for him. This included a coveted commission for the errand boy.

"It was great because if Ste ever wanted anything from the shops, he'd pay you £1.50," said Andrew. "He would pop his head around the door and say, 'I want you to go to the shop'. We'd all say, 'I'll go, I'll go!' We used to spend his £1.50 change on a roly-poly ice cream or an arctic sponge roll."

Though he was renowned for his comedy antics, Stephen's siblings noted that he was also prone to mood swings. And even though his brothers were all getting taller, and stronger, they would still find themselves bearing the brunt of his bad temper.

"On one occasion, Andrew, Chris, John, and I were sat in the lounge watching a television programme," said David. "Stephen came barging in, brandishing his expensive triple-bladed razor, screaming, 'It's blunt! It's blunt! Who's been using it?' I think Chris, Andy, and I had all been using it, but we were all too terrified to say anything. It was like some sort of interrogation. 'Who's been using my razor?!' he said. In the end, I think we all went for solidarity and owned up to nothing."

"His temper would put us all in a bad mood," added John. "But then, a few minutes later, he would always be out the back having a cigarette, and we'd just hear a knock on the window. It was Ste with some random thing from the garden. He started off with just, say, a mop over his shoulder, and once we'd opened the curtains, he was like, 'Are you comin' out?! Are you playing out?!' This was an ongoing thing for ages – he'd do it with all sorts of random stuff. He would bring us all out of our bad mood almost as quickly as he'd put us all in it."

Being the oldest in the family group put Stephen first in line for babysitting duties. But as time went on, he was more than happy to hand this responsibility to the second oldest sibling in the family, Victoria.

"Later, after Mum and Dad had split up, he was quite mean sometimes," Victoria said. "I didn't really go out with my friends in my early teen years because I didn't really have that many friends, so the few things I was asked to do around the house, such as help look after John or Becky, I was happy to do. But there was one time I was asked if I wanted to go out with some people at the last minute on a Friday night. Mum was already going out and said, 'I've had this planned for a long time. Hang on, let me ask Stephen if he's in'. He said, 'I'm home but I'll be in my room all night', so I couldn't go. So, I'm babysitting when there's somebody else in the house who could have done it. He was quite selfish sometimes. I wasn't 'cool' to him. I wasn't somebody that he really wanted to be associated with, back then. I remember one time he upset me so much that I started to cry. And I was crying so much that I just said, 'Right, I'm running away', and started to pack a bag. He just stood in the doorway, laughing. He was like, 'Ha-ha! Look at you! You're pathetic!' Anyone else would be like, 'Don't run away!' But really, where was I going to go?"

Although they saw less of their brother as he approached adulthood, Stephen's siblings look back fondly on the times they spent together.

"We hardly ever saw him as we got older," said Chris. "But sometimes, before he went out, we would ask, 'Ste, can we go in your room?' He would say, 'Yes, as long as you don't mess with anything'. So, we'd go into his room, put on the CD player and watch TV."

Stephen's taste in music was varied. He loved bands but was increasingly drawn to the strange electronic sounds of artists including Bjork, Orbital, and 808 State. His bedroom was filled with CDs and cassette tapes, from the latest indie albums to recorded pirate radio shows playing techno and rave music. And just like the ghost stories he regaled to his siblings and cousins a few years earlier, they would absorb these strange new sounds through osmosis.

The eldest of the Reding children presented his siblings with many 'firsts' – and this included more than just an introduction to new music or fashion.

"I think Mum was out," Chris recalled. "I'd come back from football training – Dad had dropped me off. And Stephen was watching *It*, the horror film. He said, 'Come in here, Chris'. I came into the room and sat down. I said, 'Ste, I'm really scared'. He said, 'Have some of this'. He gave me a half-pint glass – it was *Ice Dragon* cider. I spat it out. I was probably only about 12, in year seven or eight at school. I remember that *It* was a long film. We were watching it on TV, too, so there were loads of adverts. I didn't think anything of it at the time, but I remember about a year later, we watched the second one. It's the scariest film I've ever seen. I was 12 and he made me watch that!"

"I remember I was having a sleepover with a friend," said Andrew. "I say 'sleepover' – we were just being 14-year-old lads trying to do an all-nighter; eyes burning by three o'clock in the morning. Ste came in from a night out and was like, 'Yo, what are you up to?' I think at the time Ste actually just wanted a joint. But he knew we weren't idiots, so he was just like, 'Have you ever had any weed?' So, we went outside and smoked this joint. Ste used to have an old box in his room, and it had all his rolling papers, tobacco, and all that stuff. And he always used to roll his joints inside the box. I remember he used to get drunk, and bits of his weed would fall out. That night, when we went back into his room, I brushed my fingers inside the box and there was an inch-thick layer at the bottom of just tobacco and mixed-in weed. So, from then on, I just used to help myself to that – straight out of the box!"

§

As he approached the end of his second year of plumbing, Stephen received news that he was being released from his apprenticeship.

"He worked for nearly two years on £35 a week," said Mary. "All long hours, cycling to Burnage to get to the van. He used to leave at seven in the morning and not get home until six. For £35 pounds a week."

Years later, Mary recounted how Stephen was let go from his "so-called apprenticeship". She was adamant that this was because he was approaching the age of 18 when by law his employer would have to increase his wages to something within the realm of a respectable salary.

"It was only when they would have had to pay him an adult wage that they decided he wasn't 'cut out' for plumbing," said Mary. "And all sorts came out after that. It turned out that Stephen had been bullied by the son of the owner and his friend for nearly two years, too. They made fun of his epilepsy and used to 'play fight' him every lunch break. And then, after two years, to be told, 'Well, actually, you're not cut out for plumbing'. I can still see that man sitting there. He said, 'He's not told you, has he? He's finishing at the end of this week'. I said no and I asked why. He said, 'Well, basically he's not cut out for it'. What a load of rubbish. I said, 'I can count on one hand the number of days he's had off in two years – and once was when you sent him home when he had flu'. And all he had to say was, 'Oh, he's reliable, I'll give him that'."

Following his release from the apprenticeship, Stephen tried his hand at a welding course, but it soon became clear that the ever-present threat of his epilepsy would not mix well with the role. But just when it seemed as though more avenues were closing on him, it was here that Stephen was hit by a sudden flash of inspiration. Demystified, disillusioned, and unwilling to coast along in another job he didn't really care for, he decided to follow his own desires and interests. Who knows, perhaps he was sketching right there and then, when something clicked: he would study art.

Stephen had loved to sketch from an early age, but his relationship with the pen and paper was growing to new levels. He would sketch everywhere, from the sofa to the car, getting lost inside his own self-made universes. In retrospect, it seems a little strange that art was an avenue left unexplored for so long. But he eventually found the path, and this would prove to be one of the most positive decisions he ever made.

Stephen enrolled in a night school course at Northenden College to build his portfolio so that he could apply for a place on a year-long art foundation course. Much to his appeal, the course was almost entirely practical in nature, which would allow him to experiment with various mediums, including pencil, pastels, pen and ink, watercolours, and clay.

"He was always drawing and doodling – always," said Mary. "But it wasn't until he took himself off to night school that I realised how serious he was about it. He was working in a supermarket in Alderley Edge. He cycled there every day to earn some money and would then ride all the way to college before riding home. After all that previous job disappointment, his mindset was, 'I've tried to do it their way and now I'm going to do what I want'."

Flicking through the pages of Stephen's first college sketchbooks, the viewer is presented with a time-lapse of the young artist's rapid growth in both technical ability and creative scope. In one of the books, we see a bald caricature standing under a Christmas tree, followed by a detailed study of an old fighter plane and technical sketches of pistons, pumps, and a lathe. Another starts off with the typical cartoon 'gangster' portraits he enjoyed sketching but then becomes filled with collages of African sculptures and Asian art.

§

February 1994 came around with double cause for celebration: Not only was it Stephen's 18th birthday, but the month would also see the arrival of his compensation money. It was an ending and a beginning. Stephen knew that he would be starting art college in September, and the page would soon be turning to a new chapter in his life. For now, though, the Reding house was packed full of guests – 80 or so people all gathered to celebrate his coming of age. The atmosphere was glowing. Two stereos were blasting two different songs from the kitchen and the living room. Laughter came from all corners. There were people upstairs, downstairs, in every room, and in the toilet queue that stretched down the stairs. Some were outside, smoking or dishing out the beers that were keeping cool on the bench. At the centre of the action, of course, was Stephen, surrounded by his extended family, school friends, his girlfriend, and others he had met during his time at night school. He moved from room to room and talked to everyone before standing in the hallway at the centre of the house, where it was easy for him to get those passing through involved in the conversation.

A week after the party, a letter addressed to Stephen fell to the floor. He hurriedly tore it open and stared wide-eyed at the enclosed cheque before heading straight to the bank.

When asked to describe his brother's response to the payout, Chris said, "An 18-year-old lad who's just been given £10,000? What would you expect?"

Still, while it is true that Stephen was spending the money in his head long before it arrived, the first thing he did was purchase gifts for his entire family.

"He was very generous," said Mary. "He bought Victoria a *Raleigh* bike, he bought the lads a computer, and Becky a huge doll's set. And he wanted to have new windows put in for me. You know, he wanted to throw this money around his family."

In addition to buying gifts for his family, Stephen spent more than a little on himself. This included a new television for his room, VHS tapes by the dozen, a new bike and, of course, some new clothes. He painted his entire room black, apart from the back of the door, which he painted in an intricate wave of psychedelic colours. He also installed some plush furnishings and removed the bed frame so that there was just a mattress on the floor. In a teenager's eyes, it was a very cool room indeed.

"He kitted out his whole room, spent loads of money on it," said Andrew, who remembers being attracted to certain items Stephen had purchased with his compensation money. "I borrowed his original *Nike Air Max*. And because my feet were too small, I put plastic bags in the front where the toes go. I went out and played football in them. That didn't go down too well. I also remember he had loads of posh aftershave. *Marc O'Polo*, it was, in a green bottle. I didn't want him to know that I'd taken some, so I topped up the bottle with water from the tap. But you can't really do that. It needs to be distilled water. It went all creamy and cloudy. I was going to smash the bottle and say it was an accident, but I just left it. He went nuts. It was nearly a full bottle!"

Of all the gifts he received from his brother, Andrew recalls the *Super Nintendo* – and the lengths he would go to play it – with particular fondness.

"The *Nintendo* was bought for me, Chris, and David," he said. "Ste bought it from a friend who lived down the road, but we weren't bothered that it was second-hand. It was just great that Ste had bought it for us. We had 'Super Soccer', 'Super Tennis', 'The Legend of Zelda' and 'Mario Kart'. Honestly, we were never off it. I think that all of life, for about a year, just passed by because we were on it all the time. I remember once being banned from the Nintendo by Mum, for various reasons. The computer was set up in the playroom, and everyone was taking turns completing Mario. I was still banned, but Chris and

I came up with a way for me to play without anyone knowing it was me. We woke up really early one morning and put a load of toys and *Lego* out, just to make it look like a dump, which it always was anyway. Although it's called the 'quiet room' now, it was the 'playroom' back then, with a big brown sofa and toys everywhere. We made it look like we'd been playing with the toys, but I had the *Nintendo* controller wire running through my trouser leg. I took off my pants, threaded the wire up my jeans and spread a load of *Lego* bricks around so you couldn't see the wire on the floor, and then put a cushion on my lap, over the controller. Chris would then pretend to be playing, but it would really be me. His controller wasn't even plugged in! He would really play up on the acting part of it, too. You might ask, why would Chris do this if it meant he could play more *Nintendo* while I was banned? I think he was doing it in case he got banned one day himself. This might be the future: just terrorising Mum because even if we got banned, we could still play it! But guess who walked in? Ste. I was like, 'Alright, Ste?' and paused the game. And I said, 'Chris, what have you paused it for?' But the part we'd not thought through properly was the cushion, which was massive, just like three breeze blocks stuck together, and I had it sitting on my lap to disguise the controller. Ste, straight away, was like, 'Andy, what are you doing?' I said, 'What do you mean?' Then he lifted the cushion."

"Aren't you banned?"

"Well, yeah."

"Well, why are you playing on it?"

Andrew added: "He hadn't noticed the contraption down my pants at this point. So, he said, 'Right, we're going to Mum'. I refused. He picked me up by my hand and dragged me to the living room. The *Super Nintendo* went flying because I was still attached to the controller."

Altercations such as *Trousergate* were a common occurrence in the Reding household, but overall, the arrival of Stephen's compensation money brought some much-needed positivity to the family. However, while Mary welcomed her son's optimism and happiness – it was, indeed, the least he deserved following the attack – she also expressed her concerns regarding the timing of the payout. She was aware of the financial temptations that lay ahead of him, and continually urged Stephen to be responsible with his money by saving the majority of it for the future.

"If the cheque had come any earlier, it would have gone through me and I would have been able to help him monitor it," Mary said.

After his initial shopping spree, Stephen ensured Mary that he would not spend the rest of his money frivolously. But in reality, there was little she could do to ensure her son kept his money under control.

"I wish I could have taken that money from him and put it aside," said Mary. "But when he said he wanted to help us to get new windows put in, I said, 'You're not paying for new windows! It's your money'. And that I regret because he wasn't mature enough. He'd worked for nearly two years for next to nothing. I would have held onto it until he could have used it responsibly."

Mary wasn't the only one to recognise the duality of the situation. His close friend Ian recalled one incident that put the seriousness of his condition into stark perspective.

"When Ste got that money, it was a very strange time because he was really excited and everybody was excited for him," said Ian. "And he did have a great time with that money – he spent loads on himself, and lots on his friends. You know, we were all students, so he'd be paying for us to have an ounce of grass, hash, you name it. I remember my parents were away on holiday for a week, maybe even two weeks. It was the first time they'd ever left me and my brother on our own. We were all 18 and 19 years old. We had a massive party that lasted the entire time my mum and dad were away. Everybody just stayed at mine. Ste had a great time that summer, but it was very bitter-sweet because of his epilepsy. Literally a week after he got his payout, he had a seizure in the car with me. He'd had a few before, but I'd never been there with him. This one in the car was bad. He dislocated both his shoulders. I had to take him to hospital. It really hammered home to me how that money was *nothing*. It was so insignificant."

Untitled 21 (2000)
Ballpoint pen

Brainwave

IT'S 1996, AND MANCHESTER is drenched in the afterglow of the Second Summer of Love. By the turn of the decade, the city had become the epicentre of British youth culture, as the sound of The Smiths, The Stone Roses, The Happy Mondays, Inspiral Carpets, New Order, and 808 State sent ripples across the airwaves – a clarion call to a new generation of dreamers. From the jingle of the guitar to the bitter-sweet vocal, the Rainy City poured through the music like an audible watermark. The compass of the UK's countercultural zeitgeist had shifted to a truly special place – a place the locals simply called "town". It was a phenomenon both experienced by and driven by itself, fuelled by the music videos, the magazine articles, the documentaries, the rumours, and the now legendary musical gatherings of varying legality.

By now the 'Madchester' era was waning, but the party would never stop. Far from it: acid house and baggy gave way to ever more intense gatherings, a new interpretation of cool. Just like in the 60s, when clubs across the north west of England played black American soul to a rapturous audience, England once again stretched her wings across the Atlantic – this time turning to Chicago and Detroit. The sound of techno was on the loose. A new era of rave was on the horizon, beautiful and sinister through the heat and the haze. The epiphany on the dance floor. That pounding 4/4 beat. The *Haçienda* was soon to fold, but Manchester was moving on. A Guy Called Gerald dropped *Black Secret Technology*. The *Bugged Out!* crew started their iconic residency at *Sankeys*. Orbital played the *Herbal Tea Party*, and the crowd went wild.

For a 20-year-old student making moves in the city, what a time to be alive.

§

Aside from a few sketchbooks, little of Stephen's artwork from this period has survived. Still, his portfolio was strong enough for him to be accepted onto an art foundation course at Stockport College. His dedication, a daily 22-mile trip on his bike to the supermarket and then to night school, had paid off.

Not long after starting his first term, Stephen signed a house share rental agreement with three friends he had met on his course. The property, on Whitelow Road in Chorlton, was an old primary school that had been converted into three large townhouses with vaulted ceilings and plenty of space for parties. Just as with his family, Stephen loved the social aspect of living in a house full of people. The four students would often eat together in the evening, and during the summer the music would play into the early hours.

Four miles southwest of Manchester city centre, Chorlton-cum-Hardy has long been a hub for artists and other creative types. Stephen's house was in a prime location overlooking Chorlton Green, which hosted lively community events throughout the year, the revellers well-oiled thanks to the nearby *Horse & Jockey* pub. From the urban bustle of the Four Banks to the bustling cluster of shops, bars, and restaurants along Beech Road and down to the green, the bohemian suburb was the perfect place for Stephen to enjoy the city and his newfound independence. Indeed, by the time he started art college and moved to Chorlton, it was clear that he wanted to be a part of the Manchester scene. He didn't just want to observe it. He wanted to experience it, to live it. And thus, he followed a path that had been trodden by many a young artist before him:

> Being a student also involves copious amounts of drugs. This is probably where I start getting pretty good at getting mashed, stepping it up a good notch. Ketamine and cocaine joined the list. Plenty of parties, club events, gigs, and festivals were happening weekly. Managing this alongside studying was something that myself and the majority did. (It was a 'part of the course' – if perhaps I was pretty extreme.) The problem was, because I had missed out on so many years of this kind of thing, I thought I had to do it with a difference. (In great numbers, I would attack whatever it was at the time: pills, amphetamines, LSD, marijuana.) A click in my head and I am exported from one extreme to the total opposite side. From sensible and wary to hammering it and not giving a shit. People started to expect me to get hammered and consume considerable quantities. Dangerous? Er, probably.

Up to this point, Stephen had been open about his recreational drug use to his siblings. Victoria recalled how he gained a reputation among his peers. "He always joked about it," she said. "With his friends, he was known as 'hard as nails'. He was always the 'last man standing'."

On a similar note, Ian said 'moderation' was rarely employed by his friend in the mid-90s. "There was one time when me, Josh, Matt, and Ste – the four of us – went to the pool room in Handforth," he said. "Matt and I did some acid, and Ste and Josh took some pills. It started out with me and Matt looking after the two of them on pills, but then when the acid kicked in, Matt and I were ruined. The plastic chairs were melting into the wall, it was just wild. It ended up with those two looking after us. That night, we all went back to Ste's house. We were in Ste's bedroom and then we all had some acid. I remember Ste getting a load of shaving foam and putting it all over his face. I was, like, 'Ste what are you doing?!' And at one point he went out to the toilet and didn't come back for ages. I thought, 'What's he doing? Where is he?' This was one or two in the morning – everybody else was asleep. I came outside his bedroom, and he was on his hands and knees outside his mum's bedroom door looking at the carpet saying, 'Wow', literally, 'Wow', I was like, 'Fucking hell, Ste, get up. Get inside this room'. It was hilarious, absolutely hilarious."

Ian added: "In '95, the four of us went to Glastonbury for the first time. That was one of the most amazing times and experiences we ever had. It was really hot weather, and we had such a great time. I wish I had some pictures of it. We actually lost Ste on a hill. Yes, we lost him. We'd all done acid and we couldn't find him. We looked all over Glastonbury and eventually found him in a tent in the corner. And he was fucked."

The festival marked something of an end of an era for Ian, Matt, Josh, Jamie, and Stephen. Although they would all remain close friends, their lives would take them on different paths that intersected less frequently. Ian and Matt were saving to go travelling, while Stephen stayed in Manchester and embraced the party lifestyle of an art student. And who could blame him? The city was buzzing.

If a hole had been created by Stephen's oldest friends being further away, the void was filled with the arrival of his second serious girlfriend, Nicole, whom he had met at college. The pair started partying together and soon became close:

> I met a student of history – Nicole. We fell in love. Intelligent, funny, cool, and pretty frickin' hardcore. She lived in an eight-bed house share in Chorlton, and I lived in a four-bed also in Chorlton (cool place if you're creative). There were plenty of drugs all the time.

The introduction of the Criminal Justice and Public Order Act in 1994 resulted in a swift reduction in the number of outdoor raves taking place in the UK. But as one door closed, another opened. British dance music was entering a new era, expanding its reach down fresh avenues. Joining house and techno was an ever-expanding range of subgenres for the discerning raver: big beat, deep house, progressive house, trance, drum and bass, breakbeat, hardcore, happy hardcore, industrial, and gabba. Stephen had a varied taste in music, but when it came to his clubbing preferences during this period, it was a case of the harder, the better. In addition to attending various club nights in Manchester, he embarked on a regular pilgrimage to the Longton Leisurebowl in Stoke-on-Trent for the notorious *Club Kinetic*. Recorded footage of the event shows a packed, multi-level dance floor with thousands of partygoers and tunes that are pounding at 180 beats per minute – a true assault on the senses, complete with air horns, alarms, and intense flashing lights.

§

A tattered beige sketchbook bears the words 'STEPHEN REDING, FOUNDATION ART/DESIGN'. Within its pages, we see a young artist experimenting with a range of styles. The book begins with a full-page collage of American movie icons and the *Pizza Hut* logo, along with the words 'Fresh Baked'. Up next are the written ideas for a self-portrait project. Stephen describes himself using the following words: "Bike, Smokin', Beer, Books, Films, Travelling, Clubbing, Festivals." The sketch for his self-portrait features a male silhouette standing at the bottom of a set of stairs made from a stack of VHS videos. 'Rest here', says a sign at the top. Another note reads: "At the bottom, about to climb the stairs – into video vent." Turning the page, we see concept sketches for a "big comfy cushion chair made from *Rizla* packets (luxury)". The chair is so big that it fills the entire roof of the hotel it sits upon, and there are nets to catch anyone who might fall off. Some torn green *Rizla* packets have been glued to the page for added visual effect.

Stephen's tendency towards the bizarre and the surreal would continue throughout his artistic life. But throughout the pages of these early sketchbooks, we begin to see a subtle shift in the way he approached his art. The quick, haphazard drawings somehow become more considered, more intricate, and more complete. It was also during this time that he made the transition to paint as a medium of choice, and towards a bold abstract expressionism he would soon begin to call his own.

Stephen himself recognised the positive impact the art foundation course had on his creative ability:

> I studied art and design in several different disciplines and at various levels. I always had a passion for this. I loved anything creative. It was the best thing I could have done. It disciplined me and fine-tuned my existing know-how. I should have become an art student straight after I'd finished school, but… well, you know.

The young artist's development during this period is clear to see. Drawing and painting became his way of trying to make sense of the world. 'Eyes' and 'time' became central themes that would often find their way into his art.

In his journal, Stephen draws a link between art, drugs, and partying when he describes his lifestyle as "part of the course". He was eager to explore the fresh avenues in his mind, and good times were had by all. But as Stephen himself recognised years later, it would be an oversight to state that this was simply a period of creative hedonism. Stephen's increasing voracity for recreational drugs may have resulted from some deeper psychological issues:

> I had the idea I think that this epilepsy shit I had recently acquired, and this huge family 'Oh my God what is this?' [from my parent's divorce] coming in at pretty much the same time were leading factors in my taking it to the extreme. To a newfound escapism.

In a short space of time, Stephen had shifted from a casual weekend user to become something of a Mancunian Hunter S. Thompson. Impulsively (and unbeknownst to his family), he started to take his drug use to new extremes.

His closest friends were scattered across the country, but Stephen still had money to burn, and a long line of people to party with.

"He was very generous with his money, and in a way that was to his detriment," said Mary. "All these new 'friends' started to come out of the woodwork."

"I think I had got over the club scene by this point," added Ian. "I remember Ste joking that he had the 'X-chromosome' – he definitely took it to the extreme."

When it comes to our loved ones' association with drugs, the temptation is always there to say that they fell in with the wrong crowd. However, a neutral observer might very well say that he *was* the wrong crowd. Whatever the reader's position on this, or indeed the wider issues surrounding drug use and emotional trauma, Stephen's newfound chemical crutch would not come for free. His habits would cost him in several ways, not least financially. By this point, Stephen was spending a not-inconsiderable amount of money to fuel his late-night lifestyle. He wasn't controlling his spending, and his compensation money would not last forever.

In addition to these nascent financial concerns, those close to Stephen started to notice a subtle change in his behaviour. He was already notorious for his sudden and sharp change of moods, but these would become more pronounced. The humorous anecdotes became less frequent, and there would be sustained periods when he wouldn't call or visit the Reding household.

Living away from his family, Stephen also started to neglect his medical needs. The anti-epilepsy medication did not mix well with his party lifestyle. The raves and risky behaviour continued.

Jamie Reding, the eighth of the Reding children, was born in June 1997. Although much of Mary's time was now focused on her youngest, Stephen's changeable moods and behaviour did not escape her attention. She remained concerned about her son's long-term mental and physical health following the attack. She understood that his medication had undesirable side effects, but she implored him to follow the doctor's orders and take his pills regularly.

"He used to say to me, 'I feel doped up all the time on it', so he would stop taking them. And then that would play havoc. They changed his tablets, but I don't think they ever really got it right for him."

"Mum used to have real problems with him taking his medication," said his brother, Chris. "Sometimes he'd go for weeks without taking it."

"He would take his tablets and he'd be fine, and then he'd stop taking them and have a seizure," added Ian. "He didn't like what they did to his body and the way they made him feel."

Mary's concerns were elevated the previous year when Stephen was still living in the family home. She found three full packets of tablets, unopened, in her son's bedroom and confronted him.

"The number one piece of advice was for him to keep taking his medication," Mary said. "We all tried to tell him that he shouldn't be going out partying, missing sleep, and drinking so much."

Stephen was adept at waving away his family's concerns and often said he would change his behaviour. But despite his statements to the contrary, he would continue to shun his medication, opting instead to do things his own way.

§

A letter came through the door – *Par Avion*. The back of the envelope read:

From: Matt and Ian
Hotel Aliment
Darjeeling
India
10·7·98

Inside were two separate letters – eight pages in total, with tiny writing on tissue-thin paper.

By the time Stephen started art college, his friends Ian and Matt were already in the final year of their respective courses and had saved up to go travelling around Asia together. Their letters to Stephen were bursting with exotically detailed stories from their time in Nepal ("Watching football at two o'clock in the morning with some off-duty Nepalese cops"); comments on the attractiveness of the local women and "western babes" on the backpacker circuit; acid trips with newfound friends; and profound observations of life in these new places. They spoke of a land of promise, a place of inspiration, a paradise.

It was enough to make anyone jealous.

An art graduate himself, Ian was quick to laud the creative benefits that travel could bring. And knowing his friend was nearing the end of his foundation course, he urged Stephen to come along for the ride. At one point in his letter, Ian writes: "You have *got* to get yourself out here – to India – for the artistic aspect – you would thrive off the creativity and colour out here. All you need is an open return to India and a minimum of $50 a week – just £35!"

It's clear that Stephen aspired to join his friends at some point along their journey across Asia, as he had already diligently written down Ian and Matt's travel itinerary on an A4 piece of paper. There was one small problem: he had no money. That is correct: £10,000 down the drain in less than two years. The seemingly endless supply of funds had dried up. All that money and so little to show for it, aside from the clothes, the electronics, and the hazy recollection of a few killer parties.

Mary, who had tried so hard to ensure that Stephen put most of his money aside, was unaware of the scale of the problem until it was too late. Moreover, not only did she find out that he had run out of money, but she also discovered that her father had lent his grandson £500.

"In a way, Stephen wasn't equipped to suddenly have a lot of money," said Mary. "He'd never had any before, and suddenly he's got all this money. And, I don't mean friends like Ian, Matt, Josh, and Jamie, but friends were coming out from under the stones that we'd never seen because he had a bit of money. And he was generous with it – too generous – and then he got the spending bug. He told me years later that once the money had gone, he was used to living that life. It didn't last that long, and he eventually ended up in debt. So, in a way, if he'd never had that money, maybe he wouldn't have got used to spending like he did and he might not have got into debt, but he did."

Victoria said: "When the money dried up, he was so used to going out, and that's when he got into lots of debt. I don't know if it was credit cards, but he owed a lot. He'd got into this party lifestyle, but he didn't just have himself to fund, he had to fund his friends as well because no teenager has that kind of money. If you've got that money when you're that age, you don't want to be spending it on your own."

Not only had Stephen managed his money terribly, but he also started to lean on credit cards and overdrafts. Not long after finishing college, Stephen decided to offset his financial shortfall by turning to the one thing he had ready access to – drugs. That's when things started to get heavy:

I started dealing for Nicole's mate's boyfriend. Digital scales… Lab scales (heavy-duty, £1,000 worth). Probably dealing up to 2-3 ounces of hash at times and at least a kilo of skunk. It was going well for about six months (I always had free drugs. More money. The dealer was happy). But later, slowly I started giving less money, falling up to a couple of ton (£100) down some weeks. He hardly noticed for quite some time because there was still considerable money being handed over. I started doing more and more – giving too much out to my mates, myself, girlfriend, friends (customers), and giving too much out on credit.

Stephen started to buy increasingly larger quantities of cannabis, but as with his compensation money, he couldn't keep track of what was coming in and what was going out. There would be the usual wild parties with lots of drugs flying around. But although Stephen was often happy to foot the bill for his friends, it soon became clear that dealers are much less likely to let a debt slide after he received a beating that left him with a broken nose and a firm warning to pay up.

§

When he was in secondary school, Stephen started the trend among the Reding children of travelling to Perth during the holidays to visit his Aunt Joanne's family and revise in quiet surroundings. This had continued with all his siblings, and each one became familiar with that five-hour journey along the M6 towards the Scottish countryside.

"One of my earliest memories of Stephen was when he came up on his own one time," said Joanne's youngest son, Jack. "I think he was studying for his art exams, but he spent a lot of time with us. You look at someone in a different way at that age. He was always inquisitive and eager to get involved in what we were doing, whereas I guess a lot of other people who were older might have just wanted to do their own thing. But he wasn't like that."

In addition to Stephen's "seize-the-day" attitude, Jack recalls his cousin's talent for art. And just like his siblings back in Stockport, his cousin tried to imitate his creations.

"I was always quite inspired by his art," said Jack. "I remember, as a youngster, going into his bedroom and he was painting on the wall. So, I was like, 'I want to paint on my wall, too!' I ended up painting all over our nice wallpaper. I got told off, but he inspired me!"

Jack added: "I've always been quite arty myself. Especially when I was younger, I was always into painting, and Ste was always keen to get involved. He was at art college at the time, so we did a lot of painting. I must have been 10 years old. I always remember these clay things we made. We got some clay, and there was a big messy charade on the table. I was throwing clay around and Stephen said, 'Look, there's a nicer way to make clay. You can do *this*'. He made a little guitarist with a wide-open mouth. It was great. I made this little Scottish guy in a kilt, who looked more like a hobbit in a kilt with a long beard. We've still got them at the house. I also remember he used to chase me and Harry around, and we would freak out once he got us in the corner. He was just doing robot impressions all the time. That's something that I've always remembered."

Though he was now long past school age, Stephen would remain a regular visitor to his family in Perth. The city gave him a welcome change of scene. It was a place where he could relax and unwind.

"He was no longer studying, but Stephen still used to come here for a bit of respite," Joanne said. "There was a lovely period when he came here for a few months."

While Joanne still fondly remembers her nephew's visits, what she didn't know at the time was that during this extended stay in the summer of 1998, Stephen was craving respite of a different kind, and that was to take the heat off his situation back home. He had absconded to Perth to put some distance between himself and the dealer, to forget about the mounting bills, and bury his head in the sand.

"I think, looking back, he was in some kind of trouble," said Joanne. "He had problems, but I guess they were still latent. He came here and he worked for my husband, doing odd jobs at the workshop, and he was so happy. There was a girl who used to work in the office. She was a stunning-looking girl. I don't think they really went out together, but they had good fun. I know they had a couple of good nights out with her friends, and he just formed lovely relationships."

Stephen worked in Perth and lived with the Workman family until November. He returned to the house in Chorlton with a clear head and enough money to take a chunk out of his debts. Although his bank balances were still in the red, he had cash in hand, and things were starting to look up.

Not long after Stephen returned to Manchester, his uncle inadvertently opened a letter that was addressed to him.

"He told me, 'I've opened Stephen's bank statement by mistake' – and I was furious," said Joanne. "But according to Stephen's bank statement, he had some money in his bank and then he drew it all out on the same day. I said, 'Well, maybe he owed it to somebody'. I said, 'It's nothing to do with you'. We had a major fallout over that. I was angry that he'd read his statement, but it suddenly got me worried, and I started to think about some other things Mary had said."

§

A letter fell to the floor in the hallway of the house on Whitelow Road. It was addressed to Stephen.

> From: Ian
> Ko Samui
> Thailand

> Dear Ste! Easy Kidda!

> The sun has just set, and you know it was awesome! Hundreds of colours and shifting eyes. But how are you? I heard something about a fight? Probably history by the time you read this (unless you turn up here tomorrow!)…

> I'm sure you agree, the letter will always be best. Email… I can't type as fast as necessary, and you don't tend to sit down with a spliff for a postcard or a couple of bytes/k/megs. With a letter, you need your brew and reefer and a cosy place before you begin the adventure… and see deep into the depths of my experiences…

> At this point, just in case you haven't already, a few minutes is now allowed. Call it an interval, and I'll just watch the lightning the distance… For a while… And now a call for dinner… Shall I take you there with me… or leave you here, 'til later? The concept… decisions… thinking… Must get ready… a small writing pad next time… decide when I'm ready… hold on… I'll be back soon…

Ian and Matt had made it to Thailand: their final destination and a place Stephen desperately wanted to visit. The cluster of islands that make up the Chumphon Archipelago – including Ko Samui, Ko Pha Ngan, and Ko Tao – have long been mythologised by western travellers. They were a firm fixture on the hippie trail in the 1960s. To this day, the islands are steeped in traveller folklore, with their promise of white sands, sheer limestone outcrops, and warm, emerald waters. The archipelago was thrust under the spotlight in 1996 when Ko Pha Ngan became the backdrop for *The Beach*. Some say that this signalled the death knell for the islands. And although a heavy wave of tourism has indeed transformed the region, back in 1998, the islands were still largely off the beaten track. This sense of adventure comes through in Ian's letter to Stephen. Following his philosophical introduction, he goes on to describe a life of seemingly endless joints, fireside parties with new friends, fantastic food, the trials of dysentery, and beach huts located just metres from the sea. Ian included a small, hand-drawn map showing the spot they were staying: Haad Rin, on the south-eastern tip of Ko Pha Ngan. The letter continued:

We went to the club – 'The Hole in the Wall' (plays house, trance, techno). It's wicked. We are now on Ko Pha Ngan with bags of evil weed.

The full moon party is on Saturday, so things are gearing up. Approximately 8,000 people last month, so it's gonna get busy for a few days. Beach babes everywhere… what a shame! I've just had sweet and sour chicken and rice, a lemon and sugar pancake and 3/4 of a banana pancake, plus a milkshake. The green we've got is wicked… dark, compressed stuff… only £8 for an ounce… knocks your kipper off!

Still can't get my head around Australia. About 10 days now… and even worse, I'll be there when you read this!

And that was it. Stephen had made up his mind: He was determined to go travelling. But how? He gathered some paper and started to sketch out a reply to his friends:

TWO TRAVELLER CRAZY… How is the magical adventure?

Old School Ste reporting from Chorlton. Catching you on the Mekong! That's if Bunny has intercepted you correctly. Hope you are both well. A bit about Manchester: Still living in Chorlton. The place is looking totally cool, it's very chilled out. Lots of parties and barbecues, new neighbours, garden's looking top – chilled out for smoky gatherings, even in Manchester rain – we just adjourn to the gazebo. Oh, and a dog. We have a cross Alsatian/Doberman.

I am off the Class As. The result: much better. They had become too regular and were fuckin' me up, big time.

Ironically, the beating I received – giving me a broken nose, lots of big bruises, chipped bone in roof of mouth, made me see things a bit differently. I did not deserve the kicking, but I thanked it, in a way. It's been a few months now, and I have not been interested in the usual treats, except that is for skunk, but that doesn't really count as 'A'.

Creatively doing some nice new things – putting these long overdue ideas into practice…

As he sat there in the hallway, and the cogs began to whirr in his mind, there was a tap at the door.

Stephen recounted what followed in his journal:

Before you know it, you're £2,000 in debt. It gets pretty heavy at that point. A big gang member came to the house in Chorlton with a sawn-off shotgun and demanded the money – oh shit. I told him I would have it in four weeks' time; that I had a trust fund that I was getting but could not access it until then. It was a total blag, but it gave me some time. I was very lucky to be given this chance. I should have been dead.

In the 1990s, Manchester wasn't all *24-Hour Party People* and turning on, tuning in, and dropping out. 'Madchester' was one nickname the city had acquired, but there was another: 'Gunchester'. And Stephen was there to experience both sides of the coin.

Things had escalated quickly. What had started out with him dealing a moderate amount of cannabis to his friends had somehow resulted in a serious, armed threat. If anything could be said of the situation, the appearance of the gang member gave Stephen a sharp dose of reality. The aggression on display may seem extreme, but it just goes to show how easy it is to cross that invisible line.

Stephen had to formulate a plan – and quick. Incredibly, he rose to the challenge with remarkable precision and ingenuity, devising an audacious scam that seemed like it could have been lifted from one of the movies he loved so well:

Within five days I had everything ready to go. I sold a nine-bar of weed for £500 (bargain – worth about £900 at the time) and ordered a ticket to Amsterdam on the ferry, going for 10 days. I drew out travel insurance and went round to all my friends' houses and got several lots of receipts (digital camera, *MiniDisc* player, expensive clothes, etc.) Of all the receipts I already had, I needed approximately 10% of the things I would claim for. Five days later, I went to Amsterdam. I went to the police station and said I had my bags stolen – 10 days' worth of clothes and everything else. I got the police report and then went to a coffee shop. After I returned to Manchester, I put in a claim and waited. Four weeks later, I received my claim: £2,500. I had claimed for a lot of things. I had these things because I was over in Amsterdam "studying the art and architecture" and hence the expensive camera and all the art materials. I paid off the gangster debt and had a good time with the rest of the money.

The author has thought many times about the brazen nature of this insurance fraud scam. One can almost imagine him standing there, explaining the so-called theft to the Dutch *Politie*, stone-faced and utterly convincing. But ultimately, the Amsterdam scam would become just one in a long line of events that demonstrate the risks Stephen was willing to take to secure some easy money. He had pointed his creative energy in a different direction – and it had paid off.

§

Although the dealer had been pacified, the episode had left Stephen shaken. With some money left over from the insurance fraud, he started to plan a trip to Asia with Nicole.

Another letter came through the door – this time it was his Aunt Joanne, who had decided to act upon her concerns. She wrote how difficult it was to put pen to paper, but that she only did so out of love for him and the family. She voiced her belief that her nephew was in serious financial debt while assuring him that "as a family, we are all prepared to help you, provided you are honest about your situation".

Joanne asked how much he owed to the bank, other people, and credit cards. She asked him if he was taking drugs or involved in drug dealing or anything of a criminal nature.

"We want to help you and guide you into having the decent lifestyle and future that you deserve," she wrote. "You know that I only have your dearest interest at heart because I know what a superb guy you are and that is why I love and respect you. Call soon."

In this first written intervention, Joanne took a firm stance with her nephew. But in her frankness, she also opened a door for him to try and fix whatever situation he'd gotten himself into.

"We had a very honest and open relationship," she said, years later. "It was like something I would write to one of my own kids. I was just trying to say, 'What are you doing with your life? Is something going on?'"

Stephen kept that letter among his possessions for many years, but his reaction at the time was simply to deny everything. Rather than face up to his issues, he decided that attack would once again be the best form of defence. Stephen immediately called Mary. He was irate, uttering phrases along the lines of, "I can't believe Auntie Joanne has said this!"

With no real direction, a growing list of problems, and a payout in his back pocket, Stephen walked into the travel agency and booked two flights to Thailand. He was off in search of a new adventure in fresh surroundings. Manchester was too *on top*. He knew he had to leave.

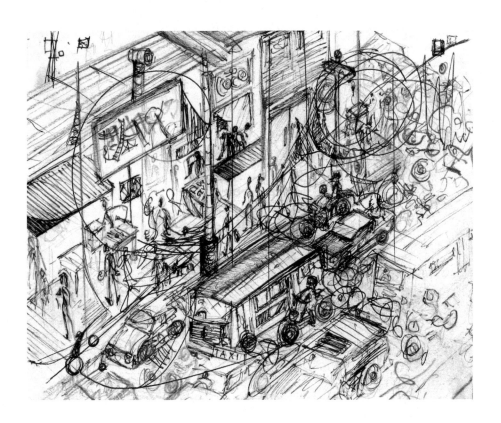

Khao San Road, Bangkok (2000)
Pen and ink, pencil

Bangkok at Night (2000)
Pen and ink, watercolour

CHAPTER EIGHT

Ōṃ

IN DECEMBER 1998, Stephen and Nicole set off on a six-week trip to Thailand. They had read *The Beach* and listened enviously to their friends' far-flung tales of Southeast Asia, but now, finally, they were able to experience its wonders first-hand. From Manchester to Bangkok in less than a day, and the burdens of life now half a world away. The plane doors opened, and Stephen felt the air's tropical embrace. A new chapter was about to begin. He knew he had made the right decision. Yes, he had credit card bills by the handful, and no job to go to back home, but who cared? The city was calling, urging him to venture forth and become lost in the superdense crushload, where life exists under the weight of the metropolis. He swapped the Mersey for the Mighty Mekong, the lilting Chao Phraya; finding creative inspiration around every corner, absorbing the sights, the sounds, that feeling of adventure. Jumping into tuk-tuks, haggling with the vocal street vendors. Wrapped up in the incense and the exhaust fumes, playing chess in the dirt-cheap hostels and swapping stories with newfound friends. He had money in his pocket and the city at his feet, sketching in his notepad in Lumphini Park by day, followed by cocktails and more than the occasional joint in one of the many bars down Khao San Road by night.

There he was: Stephen Reding, global citizen. He had become one of the thousands of young travellers who venture to Southeast Asia every year, searching for their own personal paradise. To say he fell in love with the country would be an understatement. For it was here that he felt truly alive. He realised the healing power of travel; the backpacker lifestyle was the perfect elixir for his lack of direction, the stresses back home – hell, even his epilepsy. That was all so far away now. He would meet new people every day, swaying them with his effortless conversational skills, humour, and self-confidence. This is what he should have been doing long ago. This was what life was all about. The pressures of the world melted away, as he dodged the never-ending stream of mopeds to find a suitable, open-fronted bar in which he could kick back for happy hour and simply watch the world go by.

From Bangkok, they planned their onward adventure. *Lonely Planet* guides in hand, Stephen and Nicole booked overnight coach tickets to Surat Thani, followed by an early morning boat ride to Ko Tao, the most majestic of islands in the Gulf of Thailand. As their friends Matt and Ian had done before, the couple rented a wooden beach hut just metres from the clear, calm water, spending their days relaxing in the sun, swimming in isolation among the mighty limestone outcrops, and eating freshly caught seafood on the beach. The couple topped off their island-hopping adventure with a long-tail boat trip to Ko Pha Ngan, where the *Samsong* buckets and magic mushroom milkshakes flowed freely under the full moon, helping thousands of revellers to unlock the door to a world of blissful transcendence, a world where everything and everyone was free.

After exploring the idyllic eastern islands, the pair ventured north to Pai, a small town close to the Myanmar border. Pai had become famous among the backpacker community back in the 60s, and although the boom in Thailand's tourism industry had rendered the hippie trail virtually unrecognisable some 30 years later, a visit here remained a rite of passage for any self-respecting traveller. Up there in the hills, on the fringes of the Golden Triangle, where the hot springs rise and cannabis grows freely, it was here that Stephen decided to indelibly mark his trip to Thailand by enlisting a local tattoo artist to transpose a sketch he had drawn of the *Ōm* symbol onto his left shoulder.

The photographs from Stephen's first trip to Thailand show a young man having the time of his life. In late-night stills taken from Khao San Road, we see a sunburnt traveller wearing a baggy shirt and an ear-to-ear grin, his dark hair shorn close to his scalp, and wide eyes that perhaps reveal more than just an alcohol-fuelled evening in the city. Full of youth, full of energy. Next, we see him standing proudly on the edge of a jade-green paddy field, then mooning the camera by the side of a pickup truck. Flicking through the photographs, we are now in Ko Tao. Stephen sits on some wooden steps leading from the beach up to his beach hut, arms outstretched with a smile and a healthy tan. Another picture shows him sitting at a shaded, wooden table, flanked by two topless male travellers, primed to take a toke from a giant bamboo bong. Frame after frame, shot after shot, he and Nicole appeared to be having the best of times.

Stephen called home at Christmas. He sounded happy, explaining excitedly how it was already evening there – and very hot. The kids hurriedly passed the phone before he ran out of baht.

The vacation seemed to come to an end almost as soon as it had started. Stephen was heartbroken to leave. He'd had the trip of a lifetime and couldn't believe it was already time to fly back to England. He wanted more. Much more. And by hook or by crook, that is what he would strive for.

Indeed, this initial trip to Thailand would prove to be nothing more than a reconnaissance mission. Stephen was already planning to head back once again – and this time it would be for a much longer period. For now, the journey was over, but it wouldn't stay that way for long. He was ready to take things to the next level. Little did he know just how far he would end up going.

Fishing in the Bay (2001)
Pen and ink, watercolour

CHAPTER NINE

Going Solo

STEPHEN CAME HOME in early 1999, full of wide-eyed excitement and stories by the dozen. Although I surely would have met up with him earlier, my only real memory of this time surrounds his brother Andrew's 18th birthday party, which took place during the first weekend of April. As with Stephen's coming-of-age party six years earlier, many had gathered to celebrate the occasion. In the living room, Stephen fielded endless questions from his equally wide-eyed young audience, planting a desire to travel into their own curious minds.

—No, it's not all forests and villages. Bangkok is *huge*. It's super modern, it even has a sky train!

Again, Stephen was in fine form, mixing with everyone, showing off his new tattoo and teaching the adults to do the worm in front of an increasingly raucous crowd. He was so full of life. He could seize the floor at parties, or make you feel as though you were the only person in the room. Of course, he had no better connection than with Mary – and she already knew her son was planning to head back out.

§

"They came back from their holiday and decided to save up again," Mary said. "They had six weeks away together – and they had a lovely time. They did take a short trip to India later that year but were really just saving for the *big one*."

Stephen ended his rental contract at the house on Chorlton Green. And after staying in the ever-busy Reding home for a few weeks, he moved in with Nicole and her mum, with the intention of saving as much money as they could.

"Her mum thought a lot of him," Mary recalled. "There was a point when all three of them were out of work. 'He was a worker', Nicole's mum said.

And one day he just said, 'Right, we're all going out today and not coming back until we get a job'. And they all got jobs."

It was here that Stephen realised his natural ability to build a rapport with anyone could be used to his financial advantage, as he started the first in a series of jobs working as a waiter in restaurants and café bars around Manchester. He was good at his job, and his affable character often led to sizeable tips.

Overall, the period between 2000 and 2001 is remembered fondly. Stephen's brothers were all growing older and were now starting to do the things that Stephen did in his leisure time – such as going to the pub.

"I never really knew Ste before that time," said Chris. "I was really sporty, and he didn't have any interest in football until years later. It was only when I was about 16 or 17 that I could talk to him and socialise with him. I remember going to *The Farmers* with my mate Joe. We were only supposed to play pool, but because Victoria was working behind the bar, we were able to have a couple of pints. Stephen came in and had a drink with us."

"I remember when he first came back from Thailand," said Stephen's cousin, Lauren. "I was staying at Mary's house at the time. He'd made dinner for everyone and was serving it up like he would when he was a waiter. And we all sat around the table eating the food he had made."

Although he was no longer living with the Redings, Stephen was a frequent visitor to the house. But for all the strength of his family ties, he still had a burning desire to head back out to Thailand. By hook or by crook, he had to go back. And once again, Nicole would be right there with him for the ride:

> We had got the bug. Two years after the first trip we were going away again – this time for at least a year. We got Australian work visas and one-way tickets to fly into Malaysia and onward to Oz once we had travelled around Southeast Asia. That was the plan, anyway.

Of course, this year-long expedition required funds. In his journal, Stephen says he was able to save enough money to not only travel around the world but also enjoy a separate holiday in India and pay off his student debts. As we shall discover, this was not entirely the case, for although he had managed to save up a modest amount, he still owed money to various financial institutions. He also fails to mention another loan that was entrusted to him by a close family member. Stephen was somehow blinkered to these overheads, instead simply focusing on the four-figure sum of money in his current account – money, of course, that would soon be swiftly withdrawn, changed into traveller's cheques, and whisked halfway around the world.

§

In November 2001, Stephen threw his backpack across his shoulder, said goodbye to his family, and flew out in search of a new adventure. He was chasing the sun towards the great unknown.

To the family, it seemed as though Nicole and Stephen had only just returned, but now they were heading away once again.

As he outlined in his journal, the pair had planned to fly to Kuala Lumpur and spend a few weeks travelling around Southeast Asia – Malaysia, Thailand, Laos, Cambodia, and Vietnam – before heading to Australia to find work.

In reality, Stephen's trip looked something like this: Malaysia → Thailand. The couple split up just a few weeks after they had arrived:

Nicole and I went our separate ways. The last I saw of her was on Khao San Road, Bangkok. She went to Oz. I stayed in Bangkok. I was with Nicole for three years.

§

Why do we travel? According to writer Pico Iyer,

We travel, initially, to lose ourselves; and we travel, next, to find ourselves. We travel to open our hearts and eyes and learn more about the world than our newspapers will accommodate. We travel to bring what little we can, in our ignorance and knowledge, to those parts of the globe whose riches are differently dispersed. And we travel, in essence, to become young fools again – to slow time down and get taken in, and fall in love once more.[5]

Only Stephen could say if any of these statements applied to him. But whatever his reasons for travelling, it was clear that Thailand had a hold on him. He loved the country dearly and didn't want to leave. Despite the promise of work and a whole new adventure in Australia, Stephen couldn't bring himself to swap Asia for the Antipodes and all its Western familiarity.

According to Ian, Stephen and Nicole had an argument. This could well have been over Stephen's reticence to head to Australia, but it was as though a door had been opened in his mind. As much as he loved her, he had to stay. And before he knew it, he was waving goodbye to Nicole, out there in the rain, as they stared at each other through the window of the bus for what would be the last time.

§

Stephen walked back to his hostel and started to plan his next move. For the first time in his life, he was truly alone.

He pulled out his Thai phrasebook. *'Sawadee' – a customary greeting when individuals meet.*

"It's time to make some new friends," he thought. "Let's see what the people in the next room are up to…"

Chao Phraya, Bangkok (2000)
Pen and ink, watercolour

Red Lady (2004)
Acrylic paint on canvas

CHAPTER TEN

Human Traffic

NEWS OF THE COUPLE'S separation filtered down to Mary when Nicole's mother phoned to say that she had travelled to Australia alone.

"I felt very strongly about it because Stephen and Nicole had planned this year out, going to Thailand and Australia," she said. "And what did Stephen do? He stayed in Thailand. Now, I'm not entirely blaming Stephen for that because I don't know what went on between the two of them — and if they weren't right for each other then they shouldn't have been together. But he also shouldn't have gone away with her if they were on the rocks, or if he wasn't prepared to do what they'd planned to do."

Mary eventually spoke to Stephen just before Christmas. He called from an internet café in Bangkok. She sat down on the floor in the space under the stairs where the phone was kept and listened to her son's explanation.

This marks the start of a period in which Stephen's movements become increasingly difficult to trace. Perhaps this was a result of the freedom and space he was looking for. Freedom from bills, freedom from dealers bearing grudges, freedom to be inspired. Although we often need to triangulate his position through the accounts of others, one concrete thing we do know is that Stephen's time in Thailand had an enduring impact on his art. The evidence is right there on the page and canvas. It's easy to imagine the solo young traveller diving headfirst into his work. Indeed, he filled his journals with dozens of vivid sketches — many of which were used as the basis for larger pieces that were completed at a later date. His artwork became increasingly abstract and increasingly bold.

Although Stephen had tapped into a rich seam of creativity in Thailand, he quickly realised that he would only be able to continue living the dream for as long as his funds could sustain him. Granted, a backpacker in Thailand in the early 2000s could feasibly subsist on 1,000 baht — or around £15 — per day, but Stephen was never one to do things on a shoestring budget, and he knew that with his spending habits, he would likely be broke within a few months.

At some point in January 2002, he landed an informal position at the reception desk at a large hostel on Ram Buttri Road. Less than 100 metres from the famed Khao San Road, the area traditionally offered a more relaxed alternative to the infamous backpacker strip across the way. But by the early 2000s, the horseshoe-shaped street had embraced the tourism boom with open arms and was packed with hostels, street vendors, bars, currency exchanges, and a constant stream of tourists.

The hostel is one of the first buildings you encounter as you walk down the red-tiled boulevard, passing the *wat* and the line of snoozing *tuk-tuk* drivers. The ground floor of this large residency-cum-backpacker hub is open plan, with a central check-in desk, elevators, and a large bar, along with dozens of tables and plenty of space for travellers to watch the world go by. Ram Buttri Road is bustling by day and a thronging hive of activity come nightfall, with revellers spilling out of the bars, street vendors selling barbecued chicken and fresh spring rolls, and an old camper van that had been converted into a cocktail bar blasting out 70s psychedelic funk.

In exchange for a modest baht-in-hand wage, plus free accommodation in one of the private rooms, Stephen would check people in at the reception desk, take food out to the tables when it was ready, and act as concierge by assisting them with any questions they had.

It should be noted that to work in Thailand, most Europeans are required to hold a work permit, which can be difficult and time-consuming to obtain. According to the British government's foreign travel advice for those visiting the country, "If you enter Thailand on a tourist visa, you're not allowed to work. Failure to observe this rule can lead to arrest and deportation." Despite the risks, casual employment of this nature takes place across the country, and Stephen decided it was a risk he was prepared to take. The flexible nature of the job suited him well, as it would allow him to take time off to travel or complete the two-day border run that would allow him to obtain a fresh arrival stamp, which he was required to do every 30 days.

It's easy to imagine Stephen in his element working in the hostel, putting his people skills to good use, meeting new faces every day, spending his free time working on his art, travelling around, playing chess, and getting elegantly wasted with his newfound friends. Staying over in Thailand naturally had another effect: Stephen started to view the city not as 'Bangkok', through the eyes of a tourist, but as *Krung Thep* through the eyes of a local. He wrote:

> I ran out of money after a short time, but I had made so many friends and had access to the real Thailand, not just the backpacker trail all the travellers did. I had many Thai friends and started to learn Thai.

§

It was suggested earlier that the argument between Stephen and Nicole could have been caused by his desire to remain in Thailand. In retrospect, however, the dispute may also have been due to Stephen's increasing drug use. Although we do not know the full extent of his habit during this time, we do know that he had soon tapped a direct line into the street-level flow of narcotics across Bangkok, burning new neural passages as he went. For it was there, in that hostel on Ram Buttri Road, that he saw a gap in the market: *There are hundreds of backpackers here, and everyone's looking to get loaded.* Before long, Stephen would be handing out small bags of cannabis along with the city maps. He became a middleman for the tourists, offering cannabis, yaba, ecstasy, and whatever else he could get his hands on. He was a conduit for the drugs and the constant stream of travellers coming his way.

The source of these narcotics is not known. However, it soon becomes clear that Stephen's experience of the "real Thailand" also included that of the country's organised criminal underworld. And in no time at all, he was in deep.

Stephen writes extensively about this part of his life in his journal:

> I met an Iranian guy who had lived in Thailand for 11 years. He offered me a job for £300. I gave him my passport – he would make up a fake passport under the name 'Simon Reding'. He would buy a plane ticket for me in the name of S. Reding / Bangkok to Kuala Lumpur, back to Bangkok and on to Auckland. He gave me my passport back. I would travel with another Iranian gent. He would do the Asian travel part on his own passport but would have the fake S. Reding one hidden away on his person. We would stay in Malaysia for one night

and then come back to Bangkok. He would then use the fake passport and my boarding pass for the rest of the trip to Auckland. I would come out at Thailand.

Some people from certain parts of the world are unable to travel to certain places (e.g., Iranian) – not Asia, though. That's the reason for the way that we did this operation. I probably did well over 10 of these operations with three different groups – Iranian, Nepalese, Sri Lankan – throughout my time in Thailand (definitely one a month).

The Sri Lankan Boss was the best to work for – I sometimes had the job done in an hour with him, and I would get paid more. I would meet up with him perhaps the day before a flight. He would have my passport details and would make the appropriate changes for a fake one. I was not the only person doing this. About five other Brits who were also now residents in Thailand like me and had become friends of mine. One was from Cheadle Hulme – the same age as my dad. I had seen him while growing up. Small world. Anyway, the Sri Lankan boss would meet with us and pay us a certain amount of extra money, approximately 3,000 baht, and would give us the ticket (Bangkok to wherever). The 3,000 baht was to make up a bag to check in with and for trains, etc. Myself and one of my friends in the group had this down to a tee. We would go and buy a cheap travel bag and buy several towels because they were bulky and cheap, and we would buy say two big bags of rice – this is also very cheap, but also heavy. Now we would have a bag that would look full to airport staff and anyone else, like it was full of my clothes and all other travel bits.

I would have the bag made up for, at most, 800 baht. The taxis to and from the airport would be at most 500 baht, so we made extra money from the 3,000 baht he gave us, plus we would get our fee as well. The Sri Lankan boss paid better than the Iranians. He was very organised and had connections in many places. When working for him I would go to the airport and check in at the desk. My bag would be taken on the belt – off it would go on the plane, but who cares? Not me. I would then wait in the boarding area after going through all the security gates. I would wait in the bar – order a beer and I would put my ticket in a newspaper next to me. A gent would come and sit next to me. We would talk – he would take the newspaper with the ticket inside, and he would then go and make his journey.

I would wait for a phone call on my mobile from the boss. He would say, 'Ok, (for e.g.), go to Terminal 2, Gate 44 and come out there'. This would be because the Thai airport staff at this gate would have been paid off by the boss. And they would stamp my passport to enter the country. You most certainly can't do this ordinarily. He would have to be paid off because you would need to produce your ticket. I would have a stamp departing Thailand and then have a stamp entering Thailand within about an hour and I wouldn't have even been anywhere (no other stamps to anywhere else). I would then go and get a taxi back. The job was done. I had another 30 days in Thailand (any foreigner only gets 30 days unless they have a special visa). So, I would get the 30 days and would get paid about £350 and the £30-odd made from the bag (which would be going around a conveyer in Sydney, or wherever). The whole job would be done within an hour.

I told you the Sri Lankan was a lot more organised. It was the same principle as the other job, but we would not have to travel to Malaysia and back. So, whatever he would pay the Thai airport staff he would save on tickets to and from another country. He would just buy the one ticket for me, and probably the cheapest ticket he could find for the other gent – obviously in his own name. He would have to have this so he could meet up with me in the bar in the boarding area, even though that was obviously all a front.

§

It seems wild to say it out loud, but in a short space of time, my cousin had graduated from casual drug connection to human trafficker. Readers' opinions may be divided over the morality of this operation, but given the meticulous way Stephen describes the process, I always found it hard not to be impressed by the sheer audacity of these illicit missions, as he summoned up those years of inspiration from all the movies, all the impersonations. Those films provided the perfect training ground. He became an *Oscar*-winning actor himself, holding his nerve where perhaps many would fold. But more than this, the seed was sown. He enjoyed the subterfuge. The fact that he no longer needed to cross into Malaysia, Laos, or Cambodia to refresh his 30-day visa was simply a bonus.

Years later, when Stephen told me of this operation, I had many questions. In my mind, the first was by far the most important:

—You didn't do this with women, did you?

—No, never. It was always men who were trying to find work to send money back to their families.

To this day, whenever I think of this story, I imagine Stephen sitting down with a stranger, conversing in broken English over a coffee in the airport. They were both probably as nervous as each other. I also can't help but smile when I think of that fake bag, slowly and endlessly circling around a carousel in a random airport thousands of miles away - Auckland, Tokyo, Taipei. All the other suitcases had long since been taken. And to see the bemusement on the border staff's faces as they open the bag to find nothing inside but towels and rice.

Come to think of it, they must have seen that kind of thing all the time.

§

Whenever the word 'trafficking' is mentioned, most people will automatically think of women who are forced into sex slavery or a life of indentured servitude. Without a doubt, the exploitation of women in this manner remains one of the most pressing human rights issues of the 21st century. However, the illegal flow of male migrant workers from country to country is also a multibillion-dollar underground industry. Thailand has been referred to as a "source, destination, and transit country" for this illicit global economy of organised immigration crime.

"He was going all over the world with this," said his friend, Ian.

Of course, the fate of the gentlemen Stephen travelled with and swapped plane tickets with will never be known. It would be impossible to discount the potential for foul play, but knowingly or not, these men could well have been facing a lifetime of bonded labour. This is not to mention the risk Stephen was putting himself in. He was already risking a great deal by dealing drugs to tourists – who knows what would have happened if he was apprehended in the middle of one of these airport operations.

A study conducted in 1998 determined that 'agents' were charging fees of up to 56,000 baht (approximately £980) to assist illegal migrants in their journey from Thailand to Taiwan. For his part in the operation, working for the Sri Lankan agent (and after mastering the art of building a cheap, fake backpack), Stephen had enough money to rent out an apartment:

A payment like this – approx. £400 – was brilliant money. I had a lovely place (air-con, balcony, toilet and shower room, kitchen, and bed/lounge). More than adequate. This was costing me £45 per month, including bills, 20 cigs = 60p; evening meal = 30p, etc. This is just to give you a rough idea. It's all relative.

Stephen's apartment was located just off Ram Buttri Road, with the view from the balcony overlooking the ornate vermillion roof of Wat Chana Songkhram. And life was seemingly good. Although none of Stephen's friends or family visited him in Thailand, photographs kept from this time show a well-appointed living room, with white plaster walls, wooden furniture, a small television, and a sofa with cushion throws. They show Stephen smiling, red-eyed, and wearing the beginnings of a goatee. Yes, he had credit card bills by the handful, and his compensation money was long gone, but what did this matter when he could live a comfortable life right there in the heart of Bangkok?

§

Over in the UK, the Redings were starting to become worried about Stephen. They hadn't heard from him since a hasty phone call on Christmas Day. The last thing Mary knew was that Stephen was working as a "PR rep" for a hostel and bar.

§

In June 2002, after having completed several trips for the Sri Lankans, Stephen met a young lady at a bar in Bangkok. Her name was Emma. She was a teacher from Birmingham who was travelling around Thailand during the school Christmas holidays. By Stephen's account, she was wild, sexy, and irresistible. The pair hit it off immediately and embarked on a whirlwind romance. In three hot weeks of passion, they travelled north to Chiang Mai and the mountains, before journeying south to Ko Tao and then west to the Phi Phi archipelago, in search of transcendence, soulful isolation, and parties.

Stephen and his new companion matched each other's sense of adventure, particularly when it came to drugs. However, it soon transpired that Emma wanted to take things to the next level. And so, at some point along the way, Stephen took that first long, soft pull on the opium pipe and felt all his troubles float away. He was the calm at the centre of the storm, the connection between the misty mountains in the north and the beating heart of Bangkok. He felt the pulse of the rainforest through his veins. The pain in his shoulder was gone.

Just two photographs remain from this time. The first shows Stephen smiling on the edge of a field. A sea of white poppies sweeps off into the distance. The second shows an attractive brunette, lying topless on a white sandy beach. This is the only picture that exists of Emma, and to this day very little is known about her. Can we assume she returned to a life of normality back in England? Did she remain free of opiates once the school term started again? This we will never know. What is known, however, is that Stephen took his nascent habit back with him to Bangkok.

After saying goodbye to Emma outside the airport, Stephen took a cab back to his apartment and set up his easel. But despite his creative intentions, the canvas remained blank all evening, as the artist crashed into sweet oblivion.

Untitled 17 (2001)
Pen and ink

Tropical Storm (2002)
Acrylic paint on paper

CHAPTER ELEVEN

Somniferum

THE STORM BROKE slowly. The first sign was in the shaking of the white wooden window blinds, and then the wind grew and swayed the trees. Electricity filled the air.

The rain came and the trees bent under the strength of the wind. The *tuk-tuk* drivers hunkered down in their vehicles and pedestrians ran for cover as the downpour intensified – hard, heavy sheets, bouncing from the temple roof and flooding the terracotta streets below.

After inspecting the scene from his balcony on the second floor, Stephen placed the joint between his lips and pulled the doors together. The sound of the rain persisted with a newfound *tap tap tap tap tap* against the wooden slats. He turned back to the room, casting a silhouette in the soft, amber light.

"Your move, mate."

A mushroom cloud of smoke rose from the chessboard.

Untitled 41 (2004)
Oil pastel, pen and ink

CHAPTER TWELVE

Searching for Stephen

A LONG PERIOD of radio silence started after Stephen split up with Nicole. The once-enthusiastic calls home to the Reding family were replaced with hurried, money-conscious requests for his siblings to "pass the phone, quick!" on Christmas Day in 2001. By the end of January, there had been no further contact from him. Despite her calm exterior, Mary's concerns were growing by the day.

"Nobody had heard from him," she said. "Not since Christmas. We knew Nicole had gone to Australia because she had contact with her mum, and I had spoken to her. Stephen stayed on in Thailand."

When it comes to Stephen's life over the next few months, this chapter can offer nothing more than a sprinkling of facts and a patchwork of loosely connected vignettes. We know that at least some of his time was taken up with those highly risky airport operations. And judging by the fact that he had not yet asked anyone in his family to send any money across, it seems he was taking part in enough of these clandestine, cross-border trips to be able to live a life of relative prosperity in Thailand. But this didn't last for long, and for one simple reason: Stephen was fast becoming an opiate addict.

In addition to the traveller's detailed accounts of his role in helping undocumented migrants to circumvent the border regulations of various destination countries, there were also reports that he added 'drugs mule' to his criminal curriculum vitae.

"He took a kilo of opium from Bangkok to Tokyo," one friend said. "It was like something from the film *Maria Full of Grace*. He bagged it up in condoms or latex gloves and swallowed it all. I remember him telling me that he was greeted at the airport in Japan, and they took him to a five-star hotel so he could get the drugs out of his body. They treated him very well, apparently. It was all very well organised."

These reports cannot be confirmed. Perhaps understandably, Stephen never confessed to smuggling drugs to anyone in his family, and there is no evidence of such activity in his journal. We do know, however, that after acquiring a taste for opium, it was not long before he switched up his game to heroin.

"When he went to get paid after one of the airport runs, his boss offered him either some coke or some heroin as a bonus," said Ian. "He chose the heroin."

§

Opiates and opioids are among the most addictive substances on the planet. Whether natural or synthetic in origin, the drugs all work in the same way: the absorbed chemicals bind to the brain's opioid receptors, which are responsible for controlling pain and reward. They create a surge of pleasurable sensations, a rush of unadulterated bliss. So powerful are these drugs that, when taken over an extended period, it's easy for a user to slip into a cycle of addiction, as they become physically and psychologically dependent, albeit with ever-diminishing returns.

It has proven difficult to obtain data relating to the proportion of new, or so-called 'initiate' opiate users that later go on to develop a dependency. One now rather old scientific paper analysed data collected in the early 1990s and estimated that nearly a quarter (23%) of all people who try heroin will become dependent on the drug.[6] Most people would not be comfortable trying their luck against these odds, but this one-in-four figure is still a far cry from Hollywood's *one-hit-and-you're-hooked* portrayal of addiction. Indeed, while some experiment with the drug at semi-regular intervals and are seemingly able to cease their use with relative ease, a minority of users live their lives as functioning addicts, with their regular heroin use having no discernible effect on their ability to hold down a job or fulfil other key responsibilities. Others still – such as the thousands of young travellers who each year head to the fringes of the Golden Triangle in search of adventure – might experiment with opiates once or twice, and never again.

While it is not the author's intention to downplay the powerful addictive properties of opiates (according to government data, more than 140,000 UK residents were in treatment for opiate use between 2020 and 2021),[7] it is felt that any meaningful discussion of these substances must take place in the right context. This is particularly important as we move on to document Stephen's own relationship with hard drugs, for although care has been taken to stress that opiates can impact individual users in different ways, Stephen's path from use and abuse to dependence and addiction was swift and unrelenting.

§

It was in the lush, tropical surroundings of northern Thailand that Stephen first smoked opium with his newfound travelling companion. The pair continued their drug use down in the southern islands. Heaven was within their reach.

One month on, and Emma was long gone. But Stephen was left with an itch he had to scratch. A new doorway had been opened in his mind and he was not content to leave it there, ajar. In a manner that perhaps mirrored his approach to the other drugs he had experimented with in the past, Stephen would kick that door wide open and raid its contents for all it was worth.

The young traveller did not return to the islands again, choosing instead to embrace the blissful anonymity of Bangkok. He had carved out a life within Thailand's illegal economy, and now, with a direct line into the city's flow of heroin, embarked on a fresh journey – one that would go deep inside his mind. Unfortunately, he was not one of the lucky few who could regulate their opiate use, and thus the bearing was set towards a dark and turbulent path.

Why did Stephen become so quickly enamoured with heroin? Was it his way of escaping his past traumas, his epilepsy? Was it a lack of direction? Was it a genetic disposition? Was it loneliness? Was his taste for opiates enhanced because it numbed the near-constant pain in his shoulder? Who knows, maybe he wasn't trying to 'find' himself after all. Maybe he wanted to lose himself. Maybe it was a little of all these things.

Perhaps this was simply a continuation of Stephen's pursuit of creative enlightenment. This was his self-described "X-chromosome" in full swing

– a chemically-induced change of perspective. From an artistic standpoint, Stephen's time in Thailand ushered in some profound changes. However, even if the drugs did have a positive impact on his creativity, he wouldn't be able to harness this power for long.

§

Back home in Manchester, Stephen's family were becoming increasingly concerned over his whereabouts. After several weeks of no contact, he finally broke his silence on February 1st, 2002. However, this would not be a friendly catch-up between mother and son. Their brief conversation on that Friday evening did nothing but turn her concerns into full-blown worry.

"He phoned me on his birthday, the first of February," said Mary. "He was 26. It was his Nana and Grandpa's 50th wedding anniversary. We were all going to a Chinese restaurant to celebrate. Stephen phoned me and I said, 'Stephen, happy birthday!' And straight away he said he wanted me to send him money. I told him I didn't have any money. He said, 'Have you any idea what it's like to have a gun held to your head?' I said, 'I haven't got any money, Stephen, what do you mean? I've got the kids… I've…' He said, 'Have you got any idea what it's like living in Bangkok and the police hold a gun to your head?' And he just left me with that, to carry my thoughts to the family party at the restaurant."

Mary barely spoke two words all evening. She sat there in silence, as the food was passed around and a merry anniversary speech was delivered to the crowd.

"If that wasn't pressure for me to send him money, I don't know what is," she said, years later. "He had no money, nothing. He must have got rid of his onward plane ticket to Australia, sold it or… I don't know. I don't know what he did or whether he even *had* a return ticket. But either way, he wanted me to send him money. And I said, 'Stephen, I will buy you a plane ticket, but I'm not sending you money'. And he put the phone down and left me with that. And I was heartbroken. I remember trying to finish my meal and just being on another planet."

The Reding family didn't hear back from Stephen for another few days. Word soon got around that he was in some kind of trouble. Mary had no contact phone number for her son, but someone was eventually able to source an email address.

"Unbeknownst to me, a friend of mine emailed him," said Mary. "She wrote something along the lines of, 'How *dare* you leave your mother with that'. I wasn't best pleased she'd done that at the time, because it wasn't my way. I didn't want to alienate Stephen from the little contact we had. But she did it with the best of intentions. And he did phone and apologise, so I thank her for having our interests at heart. But after that, we heard nothing from him – for weeks and weeks and weeks."

It's not known what the alleged episode involving the Thai police and a gun was about. Some of Stephen's known previous activities – dealing drugs to tourists and facilitating illegal immigration – could have landed him a lengthy stint behind bars at the very least. He was playing a dangerous game, on the brink of becoming just another statistic. Maybe he went back to dealing drugs and got caught, or perhaps he just found himself on the wrong side of the police. Amid all these questions, we also have to ask if the incident even took place. It could well have been just another rouse to get some easy money. After all, Stephen had acted before, and he would certainly act again.

Ultimately, whether this event took place or not, he needed money. He'd burned through most of his savings, had rent to pay on his apartment, and – more importantly – a habit to feed.

By the spring of 2002, there were still questions regarding whom Stephen was associating with and how he earned any money. There are suggestions he continued to engage in unscrupulous behaviour of some description, as his actions resulted in an altercation breaking out in a bar. Fortunately, it was here that Stephen would meet another girl – someone who would fill a void in his life that had been left by those who came before.

"He got into some big trouble," said Ian. "I don't know what it was over, but something happened – he cut his arm or something in a brawl in Bangkok, and some Thai girl rescued him, took him back to her flat, and looked after him."

The girl in question was Jid Saengthong. Like many women with whom Stephen became intimately involved, their relationship had a dramatic beginning. And by all accounts, they developed an intense relationship.

Although Stephen often talked of his time with Jid, very little is known about her other than that she had grown up in Bangkok. It is also known that she wasn't personally involved in hard drugs.

"Stephen always said she wasn't a user," Stephen's sister Victoria said. "Jid warned him away from his choices."

Stephen kept a collection of 10 photographs featuring himself and his lover. They portray a happy couple, from relaxing by a pool to surprise shots in the bedroom of his apartment. Included in the collection is a photograph of a half-naked Jid, with her dark, curly hair and a bright white smile. In addition to demonstrating the couple's affection for each other, these photographs also offer a subtle indication that Stephen was not faring too well. His face was blotchy, his once well-curated tan all but gone. There's a wildness in his eyes – glazed, red, and distant.

Despite the mystery that surrounds Jid, it's apparent that she acted as something of a guardian angel to Stephen that night when she rushed in to help him. During their time together, she introduced Stephen to many Thai people, and here he was able to integrate into the city on a whole new level. But just as his Thai skills improved, so he was also becoming increasingly proficient at getting high. And slowly, but ever so surely, *I'm travelling, I'm travelling* became *I'm falling, I'm falling*.

§

Over at the Reding house, all Mary could do was wait. She had tried contacting Stephen via email but received no reply. Such were her concerns that she reached out to anyone she could think of who might have heard from him.

Although she was still hurting from the breakup, even Nicole became involved in trying to locate him, sending him messages from Australia. Still, no one received a reply.

"We had no idea as to the extent of how bad it was," said Victoria. "I just remember thinking, 'How do you even find somebody who's not in your own country?'"

It wasn't until July that Stephen called.

"He rang me, saying, 'I need to come home. I have no money'. Again, I said, 'I haven't got any money, Stephen. I don't want to send you money because what if you just spend it?' And he said, 'Mum, I just need to come home'. So, I asked around the family, if anyone could lend me the money to send to Stephen for a ticket."

Given Stephen's history of poor financial management, it's perhaps unsurprising that some of the adults in his immediate family circle were initially reticent to assist.

"At first, my dad said he couldn't do it," Mary explained. "And nobody else was able to, either. I was desperately trying to find ways of raising the money to get him home."

Eventually, however, Stephen's grandad came through with the funds.

"Stephen said he would call me back because I didn't have a number for him," said Mary. "But my dad came round, and he said, 'I'll lend the money to Stephen. I'll *give* Stephen the money. We'll get him home'. And so, we sent the money. We had to go to Stockport and send it via wire transfer from *Western Union*. And then he didn't come home."

Mary added: "We waited for days, and then he called again saying the money had come through, but that it wasn't enough and that he needed more sending. By this point, I was angry and more than a little suspicious. You know, my dad had just done this massive thing. I think we sent £500. You know, we started to ask, was he even intending on coming home?"

§

Summer for the Redings came and went. Each day was spent not knowing if Stephen would turn up on the doorstep, or if they would receive another frantic phone call.

The family had come to expect long periods of silence, but now the cracks were starting to show. Things were reaching a tipping point.

Stephen had well and truly exhausted his mother and grandad as a source of funding, but this would not stop him from appealing to others in the family. He called his Aunt Catherine at the end of September, only this time with a story involving someone he knew being in prison, coupled with another request for money. Details surrounding this incident are sketchy at best.

"What happened in Thailand? We don't know," said Joanne. "There were times when he phoned up, he was in prison, he was beaten up, I don't know. Was he ever in prison? We don't know. It was like a form of self-abuse."

The family put their heads together. This had to end soon. One tabled option was for a family member to fly out to Bangkok and physically put Stephen on a flight back to the UK. That was before one of Stephen's uncles mentioned he had a friend who was living out there.

"After the conversation in February when he talked of guns at his head, I was tormented with worry," Mary recalled. "And when he didn't come home after sending dad's money, I was alternating between anger and going off my head in fear that the next news would be that he was dead – or even worse, that he would disappear for good and we'd never get to know what happened to him. It was just an awful, awful time. But after the most recent phone calls, Joanne and Cath got heavily involved."

By November 2002, Stephen finally gave in to the fact that he had exhausted all other options. With no money and his life quietly spiralling out of control, he had no choice but to accept the offer. And so, Catherine and Joanne pooled their resources together.

§

Stephen's uncle Chris had been friends with a man called Jim Hawker since they were in their early twenties. Jim was a journalist living in Thailand. A meeting between him and Stephen was hastily arranged.

"I've known Joanne, Mary, and Cath for a long time," Jim said, years later. "Chris is one of my oldest buddies. Joanne lived not far from me in

London before I moved to the Far East. I worked as deputy sports editor for *The Bangkok Post* from 1998 to 2004. I'd seen Mary's kids now and again in previous years. I remember calling in to visit them once when I was back from Asia."

Jim added: "I remember Chris got in touch with me in Bangkok. He told me what the situation was, and I said, 'If I can help in any way, I'd be delighted to'. Stephen called me at the newspaper. I said, 'Look, I've heard from Chris. I'd be happy to meet you, and I can give you the money for your flight home. We set up a meeting in a shopping centre in Bangkok. I remember that quite well. It was at *CentralWorld* – one of the well-known shopping centres, right in the middle of the city. There was a food court area on something like the sixth floor. I used to work afternoon shifts, so we agreed to meet in the morning. I got to this food court at about 11 o'clock. There weren't many people there, and the ones who were there were Thai. There was no sign of anyone else. So, I sat there, ordered myself a coffee, and waited. And I was beginning to think, 'Oh dear, he's not going to show up'. I'd been given a little background about what was going on – at least as far as Chris and Cath knew. But after about 25 minutes of waiting, Stephen showed up with his Thai girlfriend. He recognised me, and I recognised him. He came and sat down, I got them a coffee, and we probably chatted for about 10 or 15 minutes. He was a little quiet, you know. I had to work a little hard to get him to talk, initially, but he seemed 'with it', he knew what was going on. We just chatted generally about Thailand. He didn't go into a lot of detail about what he'd been doing, and I didn't feel it was my duty to pry too much. We just had a pleasant conversation. And I said, 'Look, I've got an envelope here with some cash in, which is enough to get you back to the UK. Please take it, and please make sure you buy yourself a ticket'. I remember his girlfriend saying, 'I will make sure that he does'. So, I just gave him the cash. That was obviously a risk. I remember speaking to Chris about this beforehand. I said, 'Do you want me to go with him to the airport?' But we decided that I wouldn't need to do that. It would have been about £400 for the ticket. This would have been a chunky amount of Thai baht because at the time it was about 50 baht to the pound. Chris said, 'No, just give him the money and get him to promise that he would use it on a ticket'. And I got the impression that he really would. He was very genuine. He said, 'I'm ready to go home and I will use this money to get a ticket'. I said, 'Everyone at home wants to see you back'. His girlfriend seemed quite decent, and she said, 'I'll make sure he goes'.

§

Before he left, Stephen decided to get high one last time. And as he sat there, slumped in a melancholic stupor, one of his friends took a seat next to him.

"You know, Ste, when you go back home, you need to steer clear of all this. You need to clean yourself up and move on."

"What do you mean?"

"It's different back there. Trust me – I've been there. You can't carry on like this in England, man. This isn't for you. Don't let this world cross over into that one."

"Don't worry, mate, I won't. Anyway, I'll be back here in no time. I just need to sort a few things out and get myself straight."

§

Stephen found himself back at Don Mueang International Airport, but this time the ticket was under his real name. Whether he liked it or not, he was going home.

The gate number flashed up on the board for BKK–MAN. He bid a tearful farewell to Jid.

"Don't worry, I'll be back soon. I can send you some money in the meantime."

And away he flew, into the night.

Self-portrait in Black (2006)
Chalk pastel, charcoal pencil

Untitled 23 (2002)
Pen and ink, watercolour

CHAPTER THIRTEEN

Paradise Lost

THE TAXI SPED along the M60 and passed under the bridge at Manchester Road. Destination: Stockport. The trees had lost their leaves, and the roads were typically quiet for a Sunday morning. The driver looked at Stephen through the rear-view mirror. Stephen shifted in his seat.

"This exit here, mate."

They swept around the roundabout and took a left to Cheadle Heath. What kind of person did the man sitting in the front of the hackney carriage see? This pale, skinny guy dressed incongruously for a British November in his t-shirt and three-quarter-length cotton pants. Where had the traveller come from? What was his story?

Aside from border security, the taxi driver was the first person to converse with Stephen once he was back on British soil. But there was none of the excited, casual conversation you might normally expect from someone who had been out of the country for almost a year.

"Been anywhere nice?"

Stephen was not talkative. His mind was clearly on other things.

"Away," he said.

Stephen peered through the window. From the neon lights of Bangkok to the red bricks of Manchester, this was a reintroduction to life – *his* life – in England. The green blur of hedgerows into Parkway and Lighthorne Road. Stephen took a deep breath as the taxi rattled to a stop.

The passenger door clicked. The traveller threw his backpack across his shoulder and leant through the driver's side window.

"Hold on a second, mate, I need to get some money."

Stephen opened the gate and walked around to the side entrance of the house. He composed himself for a second and then entered.

"Steph—," Mary started.

"Mum! Mum! You're not going to believe what happened!"

"Wha—," but before Mary could go any further, or even hug Stephen, her son embarked on a rapid, maniacal monologue.

"When he came through the door, he was… he was so *hyper*," Mary recalled. "He was jumping. He wasn't walking, he was *jumping*. He had this bizarre tale of coming down the motorway in the taxi, and the taxi bonnet flew up, and how they could have been killed but the taxi driver managed to pull onto the hard shoulder and get the bonnet down. And he was talking and going on and on about this taxi and this bonnet."

After hearing the morning commotion, Becky and John sidled to the upstairs bannister and peered through the wooden railings. David was recovering from a Sponsored Stay Awake, where he had raised money for the church by staying awake for 24 hours. He was sleeping in but was roused by Becky, who poked her head from behind the door.

"David… David," she whispered.

"What is it, Becky? Close the door."

"Stephen's back."

The kids came down one by one and said hello to their brother, who paced up and down the hallway and recounted the taxi story to a newfound audience. Something wasn't right in his demeanour.

"He was a shell of who he used to be and who we remembered," Mary said. "He was so pale. He was ill. He was a stick."

We had to pull over to the hard shoulder! It was crazy. Mary walked back into the kitchen to fill the kettle with some water.

"Oh, Mum, can you pay for this taxi? The meter's running."

"What?"

"Well, I haven't got any money."

§

Though he tried his best to hide it, Stephen's look of ill health was not lost on anyone. His brother Chris arrived home from work later that afternoon. "I remember the first time I saw him. He was like a skeleton, he was a ghost," he said. And although everyone was grateful for Stephen's return, there was no merriment that November evening. No bottle would be opened to welcome home the bold traveller, no stories would be swapped around the fireplace into the small hours. There were too many questions. Stephen was acting as if nothing had happened, and although Mary initially held back to give Stephen time to catch up with his siblings, she had no intention of letting the past few months slide without explanation – not after all the phone calls, the wire transfers, the worry. She would wait for her moment to find out exactly what had been going on in Thailand. But when that moment came, Stephen told her with total confidence and utter conviction that he hadn't been messing around with hard drugs.

"Looking back, he could well have been on something the day he returned," said Mary. "I had my suspicions, and I did voice my concerns when we had a moment together, but he went to great lengths the next day, and the day after, to tell me he wasn't hooked on drugs. But because of the money business and the fact that he'd been in Thailand, I was starting to not be quite so naïve as I'd been previously. I just remember him buzzing around the quiet room when he returned as if nothing had happened. Something wasn't right, but he refused to say if anything was wrong."

While Stephen was quick to deny any claims that he had been involved with drugs, he subsequently told Victoria that he'd taken a handful of Valium tablets to "make it through" the return flight. And although there were suspicions that he had taken something else at the other end of his journey, was this whirlwind tale of a near-death taxi journey simply Stephen's way of deflecting the attention away from his behaviour over the past 11 months? It would indeed be the perfect way to avoid the many questions relating to the four-figure sums of money and the months of non-communication. Stephen had secrets that he wasn't willing to disclose, but his protruding cheekbones, skeletal frame, and heavy eyes said it all.

§

Nearly all of Stephen's family, particularly those who were living at Mary's house at the time, remember his hyperactive and surreal return to life in Greater Manchester.

For me, however, things were different. I had learnt of Stephen's return that weekend and travelled to Mary's house after work the following Tuesday. My mum, Suzanne, who was meeting me there, had told me in advance that he was ill, but I thought nothing of it and was keen to see my cousin anyway. I was planning my own trip to Southeast Asia and was hungry for more stories, just like the ones he so eagerly provided upon his previous return two years earlier.

It was already dark by the time I arrived under the amber glow of the streetlights on Lighthorne Road. I entered the Reding household and said a quick hello to my other cousins who were watching TV in the lounge before walking through the kitchen and into the quiet room. My mum was there, nursing a cup of tea between her hands. Stephen was curled up on the sofa, his head resting on Mary's lap. He was more poorly than I had anticipated.

—Hi, Mum. Hi, Auntie. Hi, Ste.

—He's not well.

—Hey, James. How's it going?

Stephen seemed worn out. We all put it down to jet lag and the possibility that he'd perhaps picked up a bug out there in Asia. In stark contrast to his previous return, there were no far-flung stories of a life less ordinary, just general chitchat and an overwhelming sense that Stephen didn't want to be there. It had been just three days since he touched down at Manchester Airport, but his demeanour was far from the manic return Mary and her children experienced.

After a series of subdued answers and a couple of brews, Stephen finally became more animated when I suggested going for a beer and a catch-up in Cheadle. We put on our shoes and coats and headed out into the cold winter night.

On our way to the *White Hart*, we took a detour down Ashfield Road and across the playing fields to Brookfields Park, on the banks of the

Micker Brook. Down the back streets and passageways that we knew so well. We'd all played by the brook as kids; the remainders of rope swings adorned the branches overhanging the water. But on this chilly November evening, there was no one around.

I lit a joint and told Ste about my plans to follow in his footsteps and go travelling for a year. He had a nervous energy about him and almost immediately started to talk about the opium dens in northern Thailand.

—They just put your head on a pillow, and you go to sleep for hours. You've just got to make sure they don't go through your pockets or take your watch when you're out of it, though.

His stories took me by surprise. I was excited to be going travelling and was fully expecting to sample some of the local delicacies along the way - but *opium*? Sure, I'd read *The Beach* and had heard about the hippie trail and the full moon parties on Ko Pha Ngan, but the thought of consuming anything that potent never crossed my mind. Of course, I knew Stephen hadn't been averse to experimentation in the past. This opium thing scared me though.

I drew comfort from the fact that Stephen's dalliance with opiates was likely just a part of his travelling adventures - something he'd tried a couple of times for the hell of it. *Typical Ste, always taking it to the extreme.* I was blind to the fact that he had gotten so deep and was currently in the throes of withdrawal. And I was unaware that my cousin was just one solid connection away from developing a full-blown addiction.

We passed the joint back and forth, the smoke merging with the frigid air. I was beginning to think I wasn't cut out for this travelling game. But at least Stephen's demeanour had changed since he was curled up on his mother's lap. Talking about these things seemed to stir an excitement in him.

The conversation shifted to another subject and we headed to the pub.

§

"Hey, Ste… Ste."

"What?"

"You know I did that Sponsored Stay Awake?"

"Yeah."

"Well, will you sponsor me?"

"But you've already done it."

"It doesn't matter, you can still sponsor me."

"Why would I sponsor you to stay awake? You're 17 years old. This is just about the only time in your life when you can stay awake for 24 hours and not get affected by it. Why would I give you money to do that?"

As is often the case with anyone who leaves home for an extended period, Stephen came back to reality with a thud. Although he was grateful to have a place to stay upon his return, his living situation was a far cry from the plush apartment block in the bustling centre of Bangkok's traveller ghetto.

There had been a reshuffle on the first floor since he'd moved away to Chorlton and on to Thailand. It was decided that Stephen would share with Chris and Andrew.

"That room was closer to a cesspit than a bedroom," said David. "It was the messiest, smelliest room you'd ever been in."

"Absolute hell," said Chris. "We didn't get on at all. Three grown men in a room together? What would you expect?"

"Andrew and Ste had a big fistfight in their bedroom," John recalled. "I don't know what it was about, but they used to have a pretty tense relationship."

Stephen was thrust back into the daily routine at the Reding household. This involved not sleeping in past 9:00 am and helping to pay the bills. For a time, things had a semblance of normality. Stephen's mystery illness gradually started to subside, and aside from causing a stir when it became apparent that he had brought cockroaches back with him from Thailand in his backpack, he kept his head down and tried to make things work the best he could.

To tide himself over in the immediate aftermath of his return, Stephen sold a range of counterfeit t-shirts he'd bought for next to nothing in Thailand. But the funds from this little earner weren't going to last forever. And in light of Mary's expectations, he eventually found a job as a waiter at an Italian café bar in Didsbury. Stephen retained a photocopy of the menu. Most of the items are accompanied by confident 'ticks' cast in pencil, as each was committed to memory: Bruschetta – *check*; rocket, spinach, and herb salad with French dressing – *check*; Caesar salad – *check*; fettuccini beef fillet with sweet red pepper, cream paprika sauce – *check*. On the back of the menu is a list of restaurants that were targeted in his spontaneous recruitment campaign, along with a hand-drawn map marking one of the interview locations.

With his first paycheck, Stephen gave Mary enough money for the next month's rent, kept some aside for himself, and sent the rest back to Jid in Thailand. He continued to send money to his partner overseas for several months.

§

Despite the myriad problems he had caused over the previous year, one positive takeaway from Stephen's time in Thailand was that it sparked a new stage of creative growth. Although he started to neglect his art towards the end of his trip, he still returned home with a large portfolio of paintings and sketches. From the abstract Bangkok cityscapes to the surreal island snapshots, everyone in the family was impressed by these bold and captivating images. Artistically, it was a productive period in his life, one that was full of experimentation and creativity. In addition to the work completed in Southeast Asia, Stephen brought back with him a repository of ideas and continued painting on his return, reworking his ideas into larger, more detailed pieces.

"He used to paint in the bedroom and in the shed," said David.

"I used to be fascinated watching him," added John, who recalled Stephen setting up his apparatus at the top of the stairs to work on his latest piece.

With Stephen now back home and quietly working to pay off his debts, the probing questions from Mary and other close family members started to subside.

"Although he was like a skeleton when he came back, he still had his charisma," said Joanne. "So, although he had problems, I think they were still quite latent at this stage."

However, behind the scenes, Stephen was quick to get back into his old habits.

"Within three weeks he was hooking up with people he used to know," said Victoria. "It was just party stuff at that stage, though."

§

"I'm off out tonight, Mum."

"Okay, love, where are you off to?"

"Just to meet Ian, Josh, Matt, and Jamie. We're off to the pub."

"Oh, well, tell them all I said hi."

Mary welcomed the news that Stephen would be meeting up with three of his oldest friends. Her son had been spending a lot of time away from the house and with people she didn't really know.

The five lads had not been in the same room together since Stephen's leaving party two years earlier. Their history together spanned secondary school to the famed Handforth pool room, the warehouse parties to Glastonbury. Most would have bet on the reunion being a jovial affair, but things did not turn out as planned.

"When Ste came back, we all met up in the pub in Cheadle Hulme, and I think he made a comment about heroin or something," said Ian. "Matt and Jamie just couldn't believe what they were hearing. They were like, 'What are you doing messing around with that stuff?' I mean, that was everyone's reaction."

Two years seemed like such a short amount of time. But the gulf between Stephen and his friends now seemed wider than ever. Time had not stood still. His friends were moving on with their lives. Ian was now living in Leeds and working as a freelance photographer, and Matt and Jamie were both soon to marry their partners.

With a line temporarily drawn under this chapter in his life, Stephen started to hang out more with his newfound friends – some of whom also worked in the service industry, chefs and waiters who kept similar hours to him. He was quick to return to his old all-nighter habits, as he tried to save up enough money to head back to Thailand.

§

It didn't take Stephen long to reassert his position as the eldest sibling in the family. The capers continued in a way that was typical of the Reding household, but his mood swings had become more pronounced than ever.

"I'd just got home from work," said Andrew. "I must have been about 19. I was working in Manchester. I came home and I fancied a sandwich. There were three slices of bacon, so I made a bacon buttie. I used two of the bacon slices and put one back in the fridge. Do you think that was a strange thing to do? Now, I make a good sandwich, with cheese, egg, bacon, thick white bread, and salt and pepper. I was just about to tuck into my snack when I heard the door slam open. It was Ste. Who has eaten the bacon? I sort of ignored it because this was the sort of time when you avoided Ste. You avoided him because his mood swings were unbearable. Who's eaten the bacon? Whoever's in the house now, get down here. I was in the living room. He didn't walk around the house; he was shouting from the kitchen. I was just about to tuck into the nicest sandwich ever, when he lined us up like the von Trapp Family, quizzing us. I thought I'd best just own up."

"Who's used all of the bacon?"

"Me."

"Why have you not used all of the bacon?"

"Because I only needed two slices, Ste."

"Who does that? Who *does* that?"

It transpired that Stephen's anger was not directed at the fact that someone had helped themselves to the bacon, but because they had left one solitary slice for the next person.

"He was constantly repeating himself, 'Why would you only use two out of three slices and put one back in the fridge? What the fuck can I do with one slice of bacon?' I was like, 'Ste, you've got one slice'. He said, 'I would rather you just had it all'. I said, 'Ste, I've not even had any of my sandwich yet, do you want half?' And that tipped him over the edge. He went into the living room, looking for my bacon buttie. I thought, 'Why did I even say that?' I had hidden it down the side of the sofa, but Ste found it and brought it back into the kitchen. He threw it on the ground and squashed it with his foot into the floor. And then he said, 'Now we don't have *any* bacon'. I was shocked, it was so over the top. There are many stories when Ste completely lost it over nothing."

Importantly, seemingly every story that involves Stephen flying off the handle is matched with a positive one. Even back then, when he realised that he had gone too far, he would attempt to calm the situation by reverting to his slapstick comedy antics. He would launch himself into a fit of rage one minute before heading outside for a cigarette. Two minutes later, he would appear outside the living room window, pretending to fly around on the broomstick.

"He had a wicked sense of humour," said Mary. "Once, around this time, John was sitting at the computer in the living room and Andy was sitting watching the television. Stephen came in, and quick as a flash said, 'Hey, John, shall we practice that *Reding Routine* again?' John had never heard of this 'Reding Routine', but straight away said, 'Yeah, we can do'. Andy was giving it, 'What?! What's this? What do you mean?' Stephen said it was a dance routine they were working on. 'Ooh, you've got to show it to me', Andy said. Ha-ha – hook, line, and sinker. I was just sitting there thinking, 'Andy, they've had you. I can't believe you!' I knew straight away these two had never done a dance routine in their lives!"

§

It was no secret that Stephen wanted to go back to Thailand. He expressed a desire to return almost as soon as he landed back in the UK.

"I remember we both applied for jobs at *Morrisons* and got rejected," said David. "This was just before Christmas 2002. I can't remember why I didn't get offered a job, but Stephen told me that when they asked why he wanted to work there, he said, 'So I can earn as much money as possible and move back to Thailand'. I don't think that went down too well."

Supermarket rejection aside, Stephen had been working as many hours as he could. However, saving on a waiter's wage and with a party mindset was proving to be a struggle. For some in the family, this wasn't necessarily a bad thing, given the difficulty they had getting him back to England last time. At least this way he would remain close by.

"We all hoped he would never go back to Thailand," said his brother, Chris. "Everyone knew that would be the worst possible move."

For Stephen, however, this was far from an ideal situation. Manchester was familiar territory and lacked excitement. His mind was still back in Thailand. He could think of nothing but Bangkok. He had to come up with another plan.

"He told me that his previous credit history had been 'wiped out' because he'd been out of the country for so long," said Andrew. "So, after working as a waiter for a few months, he went into the bank and asked for a £3,000 loan. He walked out of the bank with this three grand in a brown envelope, went straight to the travel agent, and bought another return ticket to Bangkok."

As simple as that, it seemed as though Stephen would return to Thailand once again. His plan was scatty at best; he hadn't even told Mary and had no immediate means of paying off the loan from overseas. But ticket in hand, he decided to address these issues later. He was ready to leave it all behind. He might have succeeded, too, if it wasn't for one simple twist of fate.

"At this point, I was working at *Cheapest Flights*," said Andrew. "And when he told me how much he'd paid for his ticket, I said, 'Ste, you've been ripped off there'. It was an open return. I said, 'I could get you a much better deal where I'm working'. So, he returned to the travel agents, got his money back, minus his deposit, and asked me to price up the flight. It was £300 more than he'd originally paid. He was furious. He went back to the travel agents a couple of days later and they no longer had the deal anymore. So, he would have lost his £200 deposit plus £300 for the extra ticket. But, as we know, he never went back to Thailand. I spoke to Mum, and she said, 'If you'd not done that, we may never have seen him again'. We obviously don't know that, but in retrospect, it's possibly true."

§

Dejected by this latest turn of events, Stephen grabbed his rucksack, hopped on his bike, and cycled to the restaurant.

"You don't look so happy, mate – what's wrong?" asked one of the chefs at the end of the shift.

"I'm trying to get back to Thailand, but my ticket's all messed up."

"Ah shit, man. Sorry to hear."

The chef in question, Liam Evans, was part of Stephen's newfound circle of friends. They had partied together on several occasions. That evening, Liam had his hands on something a little stronger.

"I've got just the thing for that, mate," he said with a flourish and a twinkle in his eye. "I've got just the thing."

A bag of light brown power flashed before Stephen's eyes. And in the space of a nanosecond, he made a decision that would render his friend's advice back in Thailand forever obsolete.

Untitled 48 (2004)
Pen and ink, blood

Untitled 49 (2004)
Pen and ink, blood

CHAPTER FOURTEEN

Travelling at the Speed of Dark

HE WAS BACK once again in that mysterious place. That hidden place. Free from pain, free from worry, free from the untold pressures of the world. Stephen's anxieties floated away on a blissful narco-dream; his life was now framed by a heavy heroin soundtrack. *All wrapped up in cotton wool, all wrapped up and sugar-coated.* Each time moving closer to a true cosmic epiphany, but just as the answers to the universe came within his grasp, the feeling would always start to fade.

Stephen awoke to the cold light of day and peeled himself from the sofa.

"I've got to get back home, man."

"See you at work later, yeah?"

"Yeah."

He returned home, distorted by the sun, with a grimace on his face and the weight of the world bearing down once again. The withdrawals were starting to hurt.

"Where were you last night?" asked Mary.

"A mate's house."

"Oh, who?"

"Just a workmate."

Stephen shut himself in his room and didn't emerge until his shift at the restaurant was about to start. He made a hasty departure.

Up until his time in Thailand, Stephen had been open about his recreational drug use to those closest to him. This included his mother, siblings, and other family members.

"I knew he'd used drugs," said Mary. "He told me himself when he was 18 that he smoked cannabis, and he later told me that he'd taken ecstasy."

If anything, Stephen's candidness about these activities demonstrates the strength of his relationship with his mother. He trusted her enough to discuss a subject that many would perhaps shy away from with their parents.

Fast forward to early 2003, and Stephen was no longer so quick to divulge the details of any illicit substances he had been consuming. Unsurprisingly, he sought to keep his heroin use a secret. Although the exact timing is hazy, we know that within six months of returning from Thailand, Stephen had become a regular heroin user. What started out as a pinch turned into full wraps, as he embarked on progressively longer, drawn-out binges. A one-off for old times' sake became a *go-on then* after a long Saturday night shift. But then, *why not Friday and Thursday, too?* Before long, it becomes a hit on Monday to get the week off right.

The erstwhile traveller had been out of the country for so long that by the time he returned, his friends' lives had started to branch off in different directions. But the fact that Ian, Matt, Josh, and Jamie were no longer close by wouldn't stop Stephen from continuing those escapades. And why should it? His travel plans might have been scuppered once again, but there was nothing to stop him from exploring the hidden avenues within his own mind. Now, with his new network of friends and acquaintances, he was free to take things back to the level he desired – and beyond.

Staying true to his reputation, Stephen did not approach heroin half-heartedly. He would continue to take other drugs, but with heroin, his foot would remain firmly on the accelerator as he chased and sniffed his way to new cerebral vistas. He took his mind to a higher plateau, but he was playing an increasingly dangerous game.

§

It's widely known that users can be quick to develop a tolerance to heroin. The term 'chasing the high' is indeed accurate, as increased doses are required to achieve the desired effect. But just as a physical tolerance develops, so do the pleasurable effects diminish. No longer providing a euphoria, continued use of the drug now becomes a physical requirement, something needed to stave off the constant pain running through your bones, the diarrhoea, the headaches, the flu-like malaise.

Stephen may have attempted to hide his drug use from the family but the change in his behaviour was clear for all to see. There was tension around him, static storms ran through the air. "What's up with Ste?" became a common phrase in the family, until many decided it was best to try and avoid him completely.

The Reding household wasn't as crowded as it had been previously. Victoria, who was now expecting her first child, had moved to south Manchester, and Chris was now living with his partner in Edgeley. For the remaining occupants, however, Stephen was anything but good company. The prevailing memory of the time is one of cheerlessness and turmoil.

"I can only describe how he was when he got back from Thailand based on how different he was before he went away," said John. "Before, he was nice, funny, and always joking about. When he came back, he was moody – really moody. He would snap at us quite a lot. I'm guessing this might have been the time when he hadn't used for a short spell. He'd sit down to watch a soap opera and just lose it. I mean, I'm pretty bad for that now. I'd watch *Coronation Street* and would be like, 'What are you doing?!' But Ste was like, 'You stupid prick'. He was deadly serious like he knew the people. And that was sometimes scary. When he wasn't there, we'd sometimes joke about how seriously he took the soaps."

John added: "Another time, I remember he snapped at me. I went and got a *Magnum* ice cream from the shop. And you know when you freeze ice cream and then re-freeze it after it's thawed and it goes all crystally? It's gross. And he was like, 'Ah, John, that's been frozen and re-frozen. Go and take it back'. And I was like, 'No I'll just eat it'. He was like, 'You're a fucking coward', and saying I had no guts to go and take it back. I thought, 'I'm not going back to the corner shop with a half-eaten *Magnum*'. So, I refused to do it, but it was quite upsetting because he really tore into me. I was only 14."

Another of Stephen's brothers, David, would soon be moving to Sheffield when his law degree started in September. In the meantime, however, he would also experience Stephen's outbursts first-hand.

"He was still living at Mum's at this point, but he was pretty scary to be around," David said. "When he returned, he could be a nasty person. I put some of it down to the fact that he'd just had three or four years of being his own man. His life went from paradise to 'Wash the pots after you've eaten, Stephen', and 'Don't be in bed after 9:00 am, Stephen – you need to be doing stuff to help out around the house'. I went through the same feelings myself after I'd been away, so I put it all down to that. I had no idea whatsoever that it could have been anything else. I just remember there were loads of mood swings. In those days, I was extremely intimidated by him. He was a man. From my earliest memories, Stephen was an adult. As an awkward child and somewhat isolated teenager, I looked upon this guy with complete awe. But whenever he was around, his word was very much the law. Looking back, the addiction seemed to bring out the worst and best of him. When he was high, he was amiable, good company, and a delight to converse with. When this wore off, his volatile nature kicked in, and this would remain until he acquired his next fix."

Stephen's behaviour had a profound and lasting impact on David. But despite all the trials his brother put him through, he provides a reasoned assessment of his brother's actions.

"He was always so proud," David said. "It was that pride coming out again. We didn't know the tribulations he was facing. It would push him and those in his life to the very boundaries of what is deemed moral. It was a journey of the worst emotions: anger, frustration, loneliness, seduction, and manipulation. A dark path. But like most people, you don't like to lay your demons on the table, do you? You want to keep them secret and hide them from everyone for as long as possible, and preferably not even talk about them or let anyone even know they exist. He was just a paradox of a man, really. He had limitless pride."

§

At this stage, perhaps Stephen thought he had his drug use under control. Maybe he didn't think the cracks were starting to show. All things considered, although things were becoming increasingly strained at home, Stephen had been able to maintain the life of a secret heroin addict for more than eight months.

Unfortunately, the scales were tipped against him following an altercation at his place of employment.

"He was a waiter at a posh Italian restaurant in Didsbury," said Mary. "He must have been using then. He fell out with some customers who wouldn't tip him. Apparently, he was run ragged. There was this huge party and he pulled out all the stops, pulled everything out of the bag. He thought, 'There's going to be a generous tip here'. And the guy who paid the bill just got up to leave and never left him a tip. And Stephen ran after him down the street and said, 'Haven't you forgotten something?' They got into a bit of an argument."

"I just couldn't believe it," Stephen told Mary later that evening.

"Well, you've just lost your job there," she replied.

By the time Stephen left the restaurant, he was already spending more than a waiter's salary on drugs. What started as a clandestine reward for a hard week's work had become a wage-destroying habit. And now, with no source of income and even more time on his hands to get high, a new revenue stream was required.

"He was always borrowing money from us," said Chris. "At first, he was good at paying us back. It would be £30 or £40, and three or four times he'd give it back. And then it got to £80, which you would get back after a couple of weeks. Then I'd lend him £120 pounds, which came back three weeks later. At the time, I didn't know what he needed it for. I never thought anything of it."

Coins started to go missing from the kitchen counter. *I could have sworn I had a tenner in my jeans pocket.* Questions surrounding the disappearance of cash were met with casual shrugs. It became an unspoken rule not to leave any money lying around, no matter how small.

"He would always go on and on at us for money," Chris said, "Sometimes we'd cave in, but the last straw was when I lent him £200. I was going to Newcastle to see a friend at university. I said, 'Ste, I need this in six days. I'll lend it to you, but I need it back. I'm going away with it'. Six days went by, and he said he had lost his job so he couldn't give it back to me. He said he was waiting for his final wages to come through, but I didn't get that money back. We really fell out then. I told Victoria, and I found out that he'd been borrowing money from all of us and not paying it back. He even came to visit me at work and asked for another £30 a few weeks later, but I said no."

§

In August 2003, a family relative, Cedric Shutt, came to visit from the United States. Uncle Ced, as he was known among the Reding and Walker families, was the younger brother of Stephen's grandmother, Kath. He met an American lady during the Second World War and moved from England to Kentucky in 1950. At 76 years old, this would be Ced's last visit to the UK. He filled his three-week vacation by going on long walks around the places he used to roam and spending time with the family.

In light of the good weather forecast and the arrival of our esteemed guest, my mum decided she would host a large family barbecue at her house in Cheadle. Three generations of the Reding and Walker families gathered in the garden. Everyone was in good spirits, and the weather turned out to be fine. Mary, in particular, was in a buoyant mood, having just the night before met Charlie Higginson, the man she would eventually marry. Although, of course, she didn't know this yet, she was full of beans and seemingly free from the stresses of Stephen. Ah yes, Stephen. Where was Ste? He was nowhere to be seen.

I remember opening the door to him at around 4:30 pm. As his brother Chris had noted, he was a shadow of his former self: sunglasses on, monosyllabic responses, slouched in a garden chair. Looking back, it's so obvious to see that something was wrong.

I had aspirations to follow in Stephen's footsteps and experience life outside of the UK. Uncle Ced knew of my plans and had brought with him a huge map of the United States, which he unfurled across the garden table after the plates had been cleared. He took a marker pen from his shirt pocket and started to highlight some places he thought I should visit.

Given Stephen's passion for travelling, I assumed he'd want to get involved in the discussion. Instead, he just sat there in silence, in the shade of the plum tree. Ced asked Stephen a question and was met with a desultory response. His mother was far from pleased.

—Look, Stephen, if you're going to be rude like that, you might as well just go home.

Though he was no doubt tempted, Ste didn't make a scene by rising immediately to Mary's challenge. Instead, he chose his moment and slunk off in silence. I came down from the bathroom to see him walking to the front door.

—Ste! Where are you heading off to?

—I'm getting off, mate. Sorry, James. I've got stuff to do.

And away he went.

This would be the last time I saw my cousin for 18 months. We wouldn't meet again until after I returned. Neither of us were to know how different things would be then.

§

While Stephen's unceremonious departure from the party was out of character, this would be nothing compared with things to come. Back home, the situation was getting worse. With no job and an addiction to feed, there was only one logical development: more items would start going missing from the house.

"Ste, have you seen the *PlayStation* anywhere?" asked Andrew.

"Erm, yeah, I took it to the repair shop."

"Oh right, I didn't know it was broken."

"Yeah, it's being fixed."

"He used to come up with all sorts of stories," said John. "Just the most ridiculous lies about where he was taking our stuff. Like our *PlayStation*, which was our prized possession after Auntie Joanne got it for us for Christmas. It would sometimes break, and Ste would seize the opportunity. 'Oh, I'm just taking it to my mate's house to see if he can fix it', he said. But then it would be in *Cash Generator* or wherever. He would eventually come back with it, like three weeks later, and it was still broken. I never knew how he managed to get it back. If he didn't have any money, then how could he pay the pawnbroker to retrieve it? But it wasn't just the *PlayStation*. It was everything. At one point we had a pretty good DVD collection. Just gone."

"Victoria had a lovely flute, you know," said Stephen's grandmother, Kath. "And when it was time for Becky to start going to school, Mary persuaded Victoria to lend her flute to Becky, so she could take lessons. But it went missing."

"All sorts went missing," added Mary. "Anything that had a pawn value went missing."

In addition to pawning all the items he could get his hands on, Stephen continued to fleece money from his siblings.

"Mum had saved up enough for me to be able to go on the school trip to France in Year 8," said John. "It was a big thing, you know. All I had to do was raise my own spending money. Before I set off, she gave me £20 for the ferry. By this point, I knew what Ste was like, with the *PlayStation* and all that. But he saw Mum give me that money and collared me upstairs. He said, 'Can I borrow that £20?', and I said, 'Until when? I'm going away on a school trip'. He said, 'I'll give it back to you tomorrow'. I said, 'I will, but I really need it because otherwise I will have nothing and I won't be able to explain it'. At that point, it was known that you don't give Ste anything or lend him anything. I don't know if Mum ever said it, but it was just one of those things that were widely known. I was in Year 8, so I didn't have any other money. But I gave it to him, and I don't know what I was expecting. But he came back the next day and gave me half of it back. And I was gutted, but then I was thinking how I'd not really expected to get any of it back. I thought, at least he's given me some of it."

§

Although he would never be the first to admit it, under that hard exterior, behind the plots and schemes, Stephen was full of pain and anguish. For someone who lavished his family with gifts following his compensation payout, this 180-degree change in behaviour is enough alone to show that he was suffering.

For David, the fact that his brother didn't reach out to anyone for help goes back to the idea of pride. "As a family, we're all quite tenacious," he said. "Pride's a funny thing. It's stubbornness as well – we're all incredibly stubborn."

As much as he tried to hide his addiction, the entire act became exhausting. He was caught in the middle of a storm of his own creation, crippled by its grip. Darkness had crept into his life. Eventually, he was out of options.

Not long after Ced's visit, Mary returned home to find Stephen curled up by the washing machine in the kitchen.

"I found him sobbing on the kitchen floor," she said. "I'll never forget it. It was undiluted despair. I just sat next to him, and I didn't know what he was going to tell me. He could have been about to tell me he'd *murdered* someone. I had no idea what his next sentence was going to be. But it's very rare that you see anybody in that state. He was desolate. And I could see it. I just thought, 'Oh, God'. And I just sat there and I hugged him, and he couldn't stop crying. And then he told me he was a heroin addict. I knew he had used other drugs before – he told me when he was much younger. And for weeks earlier I had been asking him, 'Are you on drugs?'. Perhaps I simply didn't want to believe it. I think there's a lot of that in us, where we will hang on if somebody's telling us one thing and we really can't face the alternative. We'd rather believe the lies even if, deep down, we think otherwise. You hang on to what you can manage. And I so desperately didn't want him to be hooked on drugs that when he said, 'No, Mum, I'm not', I believed it because the alternative was too much to bear."

Mary added: "There were big changes going on with him, but you still never, ever, want to hear the word 'heroin'. And yet, how he looked when he got back from Thailand. Oh, he was hyper, he was all over the place. And then so low. It all made sense. But he just sat there, sobbing and rocking on the kitchen floor. He was absolutely distraught. And I don't think I've ever seen anybody so upset before. He must have been absolutely tormented. He just couldn't hide it any longer."

After consoling her son for more than an hour, Mary said she would refrain from discussing the matter with anyone else in the family. However, despite Mary's insistence that she wouldn't immediately say anything, it would not be long until the word got out.

§

In January 2004, Stephen's brother David hosted his 18th birthday party at Cheadle Social Club. On that chilly Saturday evening, the venue was packed with David's family and friends. Stephen was, once again, out of sorts. What had happened to the life and soul of the party? There were whispers around the edge of the dance floor.

Stephen walked into the men's bathroom. The music faded to a dull hum as the door swung to a close. The sound of a dripping tap echoed from the walls. He slunk into the single cubicle and locked the door. He closed the toilet lid, sat down on the seat, and started to cook up.

Joe Morrell, a friend of David's through his brother Chris, walked into the bathroom and over to the long steel urinal when he heard a light *plink*. From the corner of his eye, he saw a hypodermic needle roll from under the toilet cubicle out onto the bathroom floor.

At that moment, Stephen's grandfather, Roy Reding, walked into the gents' toilet. The quick-thinking Joe managed to kick the needle back under the cubicle. A shaky pair of hands quietly picked it up from the floor.

Joe waited outside the bathroom and accosted Stephen as he made a cautious exit. Stephen took him outside. A few of the guests saw them talking, but no one knew that the conversation consisted of Stephen pleading with Joe not to tell Chris about the incident. Joe said he would keep quiet, as long as Stephen agreed to tell Chris himself.

This incident not only highlights the increasing risks Stephen was prepared to take to get high, but it is also confirmation that he had graduated to the needle.

"He told me that when he first got back that he went to a few parties and smoked it, but up until that point he'd never injected," said Victoria. "But it was obvious that he was injecting now."

Like Mary, Joe fulfilled his end of the deal and stayed true to his word. Regardless, he didn't need to stay silent for long.

"Not long after David's party, John, David, Stephen, and I were playing *Monopoly*," said Chris. "And he started having a seizure. It was his first fit since he'd got back from travelling. Mum came in and we called an ambulance. When they arrived, we all left the living room. I heard the paramedic ask if Ste was on any medication. She said, 'Yes, and he is also a heroin user'. In the evening, Mum asked if I'd heard what she said. I said yes, and she asked me not to tell the younger ones."

"I found out at the same time as Chris," said David. "Mum called all three of us in. She said, 'Stephen's got a problem. He's addicted to heroin'."

The news eventually filtered down to all the children. For John, a lot of things now made sense.

He said: "From that moment on, I made a conscious effort to not think about him in a bad way and just try to be nice – no matter how he was to me. I think that's all anyone could have done, really."

Despite everything now being out in the open, Stephen's behaviour did not change. When he was home, he was usually in bed, occasionally heading outside for a cigarette before going to meet a friend. Sometimes he would go missing for days on end. And when he came back, things were usually even worse than before.

"Stephen's rages were a thing of beauty. But not when you were on the receiving end," said Chris. "We were all scared of him turning on us, over little things like a phone charger. He went mental at me once. I said one off-the-cuff comment that I could get a spare phone charger if he wanted it. He said yes. Three days later it was, 'Where's this charger? Where is it, where is it?' He went crazy wanting to know where it was."

Stephen had always been prone to mood swings, but things were now taking a more sinister turn. These were comedowns on the scale of nuclear winter. Long gone were the days when he would use his charm to explain away his actions the following day.

The family's accounts of Stephen's character during this time range from ludicrous to downright scary.

"He used to really get on Becky's case," John said. "Becky had courage. We were all pretty scared of him. And she would argue with him. And Ste would go mad. She would never back down. David, Chris, and I would be like, 'Bloody hell, Becky, just leave it'."

For David, one incident illustrates just how far Stephen's descent into darkness had gone. It had such an impact on David that he wrote it down in his journal:

With Stephen, the banal became the most important. Whatever his mind was focused on took hold of him. If issues weren't resolved according to his confused and unreasonable agenda, then his tongue became vicious. He was a man who could articulate words with an ease and elegance that few are bestowed with. This was his blessing and curse. For Stephen, it gave him a charm and charisma that led people to him. For his heroin, it gave him a dark, scary weapon.

In April 2004, Mum and I needed to attend a Lourdes meeting at the church, but there was no one at home to look after Jamie. Stephen had been in Stockport, doing whatever he was doing, and Mum demanded that he returned home promptly. Stephen said he was walking back, to which Mum retorted he should get on the first bus home. He did. However, in the meantime, Chris returned from work and the need for the oldest to return home was made redundant.

Understandably irked, he savagely turned on me later that evening. He had decided that as we had cost him his bus fare, we owed him the money – and that it was my duty to give him my bus pass. It wasn't stated as a suggestion: it was demanded. Up until this point I had always avoided the full extent of his wrath. But it was my time to receive, and I stood up for myself. It was the first time I stood up to him after months of spinelessly bending to his will. 'No, Stephen, it's mine. If you have an issue with getting the bus, get money from Mum'. This truly set him over the edge. His words were unrelenting in their aggression and always framed with the most perfect diction. There were many words thrown in my direction, the potency of which were so intense that the adrenaline hazes my memory. One excerpt that I do remember is, 'You pathetic waste, look at you, sulking always, stand up – I can see it in your useless eyes you want to cry. You don't agree with my reasoning? Stand up for yourself'. I was terrified. I eventually threw the bus pass in his direction and said, 'Fine, have it, you bully'. I stormed upstairs, drained and tear-strewn. I waited. The second round was imminent. Sure enough, the stairs boomed, and the door flew open. 'Loser! Ha-ha! Are you crying?! Just letting you know that if you sneak the bus pass out of my pocket in the morning, you're a dead man. I'll leave you to cry now'.

Whether Mum ever found out, or if I ever got the bus the next morning, is unclear. In his wake, he left a path of pure terror. The above took place in front of John, Chris, and Andrew. It wasn't even humiliating to be exposed so ruthlessly in front of them. They all knew what I was experiencing. They were there for me. We took solace from each other. On occasion, we would tell Mum of the incidents that took place. She was his rock, and I suppose without her he would have gone down an even slipperier road. Not that we thought like that at the time.

In addition to making his mother and siblings' lives a misery, Stephen's descent into addiction had started to impact people outside the family. On more than one occasion, Mary had to answer the door to friends and acquaintances who were looking for her son because he owed them money or had something of theirs. She had nothing else to say to them other than: "You won't see that money again. Stephen is a heroin addict."

There are many tales of Stephen's actions during this time. He committed a multitude of wrongdoings to those closest to him. At the request of some, these stories will not be recounted here. However, one further stark indicator of Stephen's demeanour took place when he directed his venom towards his own mother – the one person who had been so sympathetic and accommodating.

"Mum is an amazing woman," said John. "We never really fall out. And she had done so much for everybody. One day she received a card from a friend. It was a card saying how brilliant Mum was and thanking her for helping her out in Lourdes. Ste picked up this card and read it. He just threw it down onto the floor and said, 'Saint. Fucking. Mum. Always pleasing everyone else'."

§

Stephen tried to keep it together. He tried his best to get his life under control. But by this point, his actions were akin to rearranging the deck chairs on the *Titanic*. Any positive changes went out of the window as soon as the hunger set in.

No one in the family was equipped to deal with his addiction – least of all Stephen. But things eventually reached a tipping point. Something had to give.

"It wasn't *Stephen*," said Chris. "It wasn't him. It was horrible to live with and horrible to see. It got to the point where it was unbearable. Mum said he had to go. She'd had enough. I had already moved out by this time. I didn't want to know him. It's horrible to say, but I just didn't want to know him. He'd go from politely asking for money to screaming in your face."

Stephen had spun a web of lies and had stolen from the people closest to him. But of all the incidents that took place as he ran circles around the Redings, the one incident that prompted Mary to ask him to leave involved his art.

"It was partly due to the fact that I had Jamie and the others to look after, but it was also because I absolutely refused to give him another penny," said Mary. "I said, 'It's got to stop. If you can't fit into the family life we're trying to get going here – the life you had when you were a kid, which I want all my kids to have – this isn't the place for you. If you can't accept the kind of help that I want to give you, then you have to leave."

She added: "He tried to sell me some paintings of his. I agreed, in principle, but when he showed them to me, it was obvious that there were just cheap photocopies that he'd put in little frames. He said, 'Choose as many as you want, Mum'. No money had been mentioned by this point, so I picked four and he said, 'Right, that's £40 you owe me'. And I was like, 'Well I haven't got £40, you're having a laugh'. And he said, 'Okay, because you're my mum, I'll let you have them all for £30'. And I thought, 'This is wrong, this is so wrong'. He'd just whizzed them off for five pence a copy at the newsagents. I thought, 'All I'm doing is giving you your drug money'. And I said, 'This is the last time I part money for you'."

Stephen left the house in June 2004. This was not, of course, a decision Mary took lightly, but after seeing this once passionate artist disrespecting his own work in this way, it was a bridge too far.

"I said, 'I'm not doing it anymore, because really I may as well be just handing you thirty pounds and letting you go and get what you want'. I said, 'It's got to stop, and it stops here'. And he left. And I never saw him again – not for months."

Aware of the vast amount of pressure her sister had been under, Joanne commended Mary for the way she handled the situation.

"The thing is, everyone had to be so careful," she said. "You can't live your life like that. He had been given a chance, and Mary was amazing. I had no idea how she kept so strong. I can't imagine how anybody could be as strong as she was. The strength came with her saying, 'I'm sorry, you cannot live in this house. I have young children. You can live in this house if you agree not to use drugs. If not, you have to leave'. We know what an open and caring person she is. She opened her arms to Stephen, but he simply couldn't stop using."

Untitled 54 (2005)
Pencil

CHAPTER FIFTEEN

Buried Treasure

NOW ABSENT FROM his family, Stephen continued on a path of self-destruction, one that was lined with chaos, confusion, and drugs. Lies and deceit were the new orders of service. He was starting to lose control.

One may wonder if Stephen ever doubted his own actions during this time. Did he ever question his increasingly chaotic lifestyle? It's perhaps difficult to imagine anyone living such a life without realising the damage they were causing to themselves and those around them. But even if Stephen did make intermittent efforts to reduce his heroin use, the self-made promises of the night before soon melted away into the ether. Come morning, the ritual continued: *Water in the syringe. Heroin in the spoon. The tiniest drop of heaven. One more hit and I'll get clean.*

After spending some time sleeping on the sofa at the homes of various acquaintances, Stephen rekindled a relationship with an ex-girlfriend whom he had dated during his teenage years. This relationship will not be discussed in detail, but it should be noted that this young woman also felt the impact of Stephen's addiction. She tried to help him, but he took advantage of that trust. Used needles were found stashed around the house. Her belongings were stolen for drug money. If this wasn't grounds for her to turf him out then nothing was, but it always seemed that before anyone had the chance to accost Stephen or – worse still, in his mind – launch another intervention, he was gone. He cut himself adrift and disappeared over the horizon once again.

Stephen's chosen family during this time consisted of other users. And in this new fraternity, he attacked the drugs with a newfound zeal. Before long, rocks were thrown into the mix. And that's when things really started to crumble.

Just as we don't know exactly when Stephen transitioned from smoking heroin to picking up the needle, so it's unclear when crack was added to his narcotics playlist. We do know that once he had sampled that otherworldly combination – the cocaine freight train followed by the opiate euphoria – there was no going back. Over the years, he had tried almost every recreational drug out there, but nothing could beat the power of a speedball. And so, whereabouts unknown, Stephen slipped further into a drug-induced stupor, going deeper into the heart of his own, personal *Kali Yuga*.

Polysubstance abuse does not come cheap. At this stage, Stephen was estimated to have been spending at least £40 a day just to keep himself on a level footing – and plenty more if he really wanted to get loose. With no job, it would only be logical to assume he had been acquiring a lot of debt. However, Stephen's financial situation was far worse than anyone could have imagined. Amid the sea of uncertainty surrounding his life during this time, one thing we are not forced to speculate on was his financial status, thanks to a folder he retained that was full of bank letters and statements.

The earliest of these letters dates back to June 2003, when Stephen's finances started to take a relentless downward turn. On June 19th his *HSBC* current account statement shows a balance of £2,074 being reduced to just £11.42 following a loan repayment. (How he managed to have such a large opening balance soon becomes clear.) Instead of eating into his overdraft, Stephen turned to other, less reputable sources:

SHOPACHECK FINANCIAL SERVICES
68 Turn Moss Lane
Hull
HU14 6GG

Date: 3rd July 2003

Dear Mr Reding,

I am delighted to welcome you as a Shopacheck customer, and I have enclosed a leaflet which gives full details of the wide range of products and services we have available.

In addition, I have enclosed your payment book and would draw your attention to the customer information on the inside front cover regarding payment of your account.

If you would like any further information, please do not hesitate to give me a call.

Yours sincerely,

[Redacted]

Branch Manager

Shopacheck was a high street 'payday loan' business offering quick and easy loans to cash-strapped British consumers. The only catch was the hefty surcharge attached to each withdrawal. Further charges would be heaped onto the accounts of late-paying customers. Stephen's account book showed an initial *Shopacheck* loan of £500, which came with a large £295 fee, giving a grand total of £795 to be paid in instalments of £26.50 a week for 30 weeks.

Given his limited means and patchy financial history, one might ask how Stephen could have been accepted for a loan in the first place. But during this time, before the global financial crisis of 2008, lenders were handing out money with very little regard for their customers' long-term financial situation. This, combined with the fact that Stephen used his mother's address when taking out these loans, made getting into debt a trivial exercise.

All things considered, and despite the near-50% surcharge, £795 wasn't the biggest debt in the world. This loan, however, does little to describe the full extent of Stephen's financial situation. One month later, another letter reveals that he had a second account with *HSBC* – a 'managed loan account'. Here, it becomes apparent that things were a lot worse:

HSBC Bank Plc
Customer Credit Services
P.O. Box 1681
Sheffield
S2 4US

01 AUG 2003

Our Ref: 401886 51240107

Parties: Mr S J Reding

Default Notice served under Section 81(1) of
The Consumer Credit Act 1974 .
IMPORTANT – YOU SHOULD READ THIS CAREFULLY

This notice refers to a credit agreement regulated by the Consumer Credit Act 1974 under Account No. 51230107.

Term Breached: The term or terms of the agreement form requiring you to make payments.

Nature of Breach: Failure to make payments as required under the agreement.

Amount owing, including interest and charges up to 1st August 2003: £5,640.49.

Yours sincerely,

[Redacted]

Manager

This large loan of more than £5,600 explains why Stephen didn't first use his current account overdraft facility before taking out any other loans: the bank had more than likely cut him off weeks ago.

The *Shopacheck* loan had come through, but just two days after the default notice from *HSBC*, Stephen received another letter. This one marked a shift in tone:

SHOPACHECK FINANCIAL SERVICES
68 Turn Moss Lane
Hull
HU14 6GG

Date: 28th August 2003

Dear Mr Reding,

The enclosed cheque, which we recently accepted from you as payment against your account, has been returned by the bank marked 'refer to drawer'. This means that there were insufficient funds in your account for the bank to pay us.

Our bank makes a charge to us for all such cheques and, therefore, we have debited your account with the amount of the cheque plus a fee of £11.00 to cover administrative costs.

We should point out that this is an expensive exercise for both parties. You should, therefore, make certain that there are sufficient funds in your account to meet any further cheques you draw.

Yours sincerely,

[Redacted]

Branch Manager

From this point onwards, following Stephen's paper trail becomes a dizzying exercise. One further letter indicates that Stephen had taken out another loan, which he was also failing to honour:

This letter is sent about your
Egg Card

It was sent to you on
30 August 2003

Egg Card number
6427 8540 0312 7494

Dear Mr Reding,

I am disappointed to note that your Direct Debit instruction for your monthly payment has been cancelled. To correct this situation can you please set up a new Direct Debit mandate in time for next month's payment.

I would point out that the Egg Card terms and conditions provide that your monthly payment must be made by Direct Debit, and we reserve the right to charge administration fees for payments not cleared.

Yours sincerely,

[Redacted]

Account Handler, egg.com

The amount taken out with *Egg* is unknown, but this letter offers clear evidence that Stephen was taking out loans to pay off other loans. His unusually high opening balance at the beginning of June 2003 was obliterated by a large loan repayment. By August 22nd his balance was back to nil. The hole he was digging was getting bigger. Following a further warning letter from *Shopacheck* on August 28th, another lender entered the scene:

The Money Shop
Circle Lane
Northampton
NN7 1QD

12 September 2003

Our ref: DETNFC/BAL/998622

Dear Stephen Reding,

This is a DEFAULT NOTICE
Served under Section 87(1) of the Consumer Credit Act 1974

In respect of a loan agreement made between you, Stephen Reding, of the above address, and The Money Shop ("the company").

The following breach of the above agreement has taken place: **FAILURE TO MAKE PAYMENT TO THE MONEY SHOP**.

To remedy this breach, you are required to take the following action **within 7 DAYS FROM DATE OF POSTMARK**.

Action required: BALANCE OF THE ACCOUNT IN FULL £285.00 paid to The Money Shop, to clear the debt on your account.

IF THE ACTION REQUIRED BY THIS NOTICE IS TAKEN **BEFORE THE DATE SHOWN**, NO FURTHER ENFORCEMENT ACTION WILL BE TAKEN IN RESPECT OF THE BREACH. IF YOU DO NOT TAKE THE ACTION REQUIRED **BEFORE THE DATE SHOWN, THEN FURTHER ACTION SET OUT BELOW MAY BE TAKEN AGAINST YOU**.

Yours sincerely,

[Redacted]

Collections Department

His list of debts was seemingly never-ending. September 24th was a particularly grim day, as Stephen received letters from two different lenders. These notices took an increasingly demanding tone. *YOUR ARREARS HAVE RISEN TO AN UNACCEPTABLE LEVEL. IT'S NOT TOO LATE TO RESOLVE THIS PROBLEM. PRE-LEGAL NOTICE. PAY THE DEBT IN FULL.* Stephen's inglorious attempt to hawk cheap photocopies of his artwork to his mother for £40 now starts to make a little more sense. He was playing a balancing act with his finances; one break in the chain was all that was needed for everything to come crashing down. And in what had become a familiar theme in Stephen's life, he buried his head in the sand instead of letting someone know he was in trouble. The situation is even more unfortunate given that he started out with more than £10,000 following his compensation payout just a few years earlier.

Among Stephen's paperwork and financial statements were two A4 pieces of paper, on which we see him try to bring some order to his financial situation. His notes read like a veritable shopping list of payments: *Shopacheck (£26.50), Money Bank (£50 per week, Friday), Cash Generator (£50), Egg (£65), HSBC Loan Arrears (£170), Overdraft (-£187.82).* At the foot of one of the pieces of paper, below an entry for his brother – *David (£50)* – and a haphazard sketch of a face with a wide-open mouth, two new individuals enter the scene: 'Paul' and 'Jester', who were owed £300 and £110, respectively. It's not hard to guess who these friends were, and, of all the lenders, who would be getting their money back first.

During the summer of 2004, Stephen declared himself homeless and was placed on the waiting list for accommodation in the Stockport area. When it came to addressing his immediate financial situation, it was perhaps fortunate that his social circle consisted of fellow addicts, some of whom took a less-than-traditional approach to earning a living. And it was here, with all sources of legitimate funds exhausted, that Stephen decided to look for cash elsewhere on the high street. In this loosely formed collective of ne'er-do-wells, he shunned the *Job Centre* in favour of a different career.

"It was so easy, Victoria," he told his sister, years later, as he described the ins and outs of what he euphemistically called 'grafting'. Though he had been denied a job at *Morrisons* months earlier, supermarkets became a strong earner for Stephen, as he plundered the shelves in broad daylight. Department stores also offered easy pickings for the young junkie, who would leverage his experience on the wrong side of the law to his benefit. He had previously bluffed his way through police interviews. Hell, there were even rumours he'd smuggled drugs into Japan. Stealing from a store was child's play.

"I was down the wines and spirits aisle once, and a lady on the checkout counter saw me put a litre bottle of vodka inside my coat," he told Victoria. "I just looked her straight in the eye and carried on as if everything was normal. I never got caught there."

§

Although Stephen had distanced himself from his family, he wasn't entirely isolated. Victoria would remain an intermediary of sorts, speaking to him on the phone occasionally and passing on the details to Mary. At one point he reached out to his brother, Andrew, but perhaps understandably, Andrew was hesitant to comply with his requests.

"To be honest, I distanced myself from Ste for a few months," Andrew said. "He went off the rails. I was living in Reddish. I was house-sharing with a mate, and I got a call from Ste. He said, 'Alright, Andy? Is there any chance I can stay over?' This was after him borrowing all that money and never paying anyone back. I think he owed me £300 or £400. And the first thing I thought was, 'It's not my TV in this house, it's not my DVD player'. And I said, 'No'. And I regret that. Ste said, 'Okay, I'll just have to inquire at the homeless shelter then. Don't worry about it'. I felt awful because I loved him to bits. But all our electronic equipment had just disappeared. It was just an impossible situation."

Victoria also found herself torn between wanting to help her brother and having to keep him at arm's length. She would remain the family's primary point of contact during this troubled time. Still, despite her efforts to help him get clean, she also found herself the focus of his money-making schemes as he took increasingly desperate measures to feed his addiction.

One day, Stephen showed up at her door.

"It was at the stage where he'd do anything to get money," said David. "Victoria was pregnant. He was in the phase where he was just taking everything, anything he could get cash for. He saw value in things that had no value. He was at Victoria's house and said, 'I see your VHS videos there. You can get 50p for each of those in *Cash Converters*'. She used to have loads of videos – the entire *Friends* collection and lots more."

"I don't even want to sell them," Victoria said. "And how on earth do you expect me to take every single one of these videos in my state?"

"Oh, it's alright, we'll do separate trips."

"Not a chance."

Although Victoria would not be persuaded to part with her VHS tapes, Stephen pleaded with her to lend him some money.

"That same day in 2004, Victoria called me," added David. "She asked me if I wanted to come over for tea. When I got there, she said, 'David, I need a favour. I'm desperate. Can I borrow £150 for my rent?' This was strange because Victoria has always been quite frugal. I said, 'Sure, but why?' She said, 'Well, I've just seen Stephen'. Apparently, she'd let it slip that the rent money was in the cookie jar. And once he'd heard that, dollar signs lit up in his eyes like a fruit machine. God, to go through all that – especially when you're pregnant. It was a terrible mess. That was the last time she invited him into the house for a long time."

It will come as no surprise to learn that after grasping the rent money from his sister's hands, Stephen once again disappeared into the distance. He ignored any further phone calls from his family and, once again, retreated from public view. There were scattered reports of his whereabouts as summer came to an end. He was twice seen slinking around Stockport, but both times hurried off out of sight. On one occasion, Mary entered the church hall following the Sunday service, and the priest informed her that Stephen had been found sleeping on the church porch when they came to open in the morning.

This latest spell of non-communication was broken in October, as Victoria was able to get in touch with Stephen to inform him that his grandfather, Charles West, had passed away. Grandad West, the man who loved his family so dearly. The man who cherished Stephen as a child. The man who had helped the Reding family through so much. Gentle Charlie, who was famed for his extended goodbyes and his warm, pipe tobacco hug.

The family came together on October 14th. It had been weeks since Becky had last seen her brother, and she remembers the day clearly.

"Stephen was still missing, but Victoria managed to get hold of him," Becky said. "Mum woke us up early hours Tuesday to tell us about Grandad, and Stephen was there. He was sitting in the garden. He just sat there with his head in his hands. He was very quiet."

Joanne, who had driven down from Perth earlier in the week, also recalls Stephen's sombre reintroduction to the family.

"There had been a huge blow-up between him and Mary, and he'd disappeared," she said. "We didn't know where he was. We heard he'd been homeless. A couple of days before my dad's funeral, we all went on a walk. And when we came back, I remember Stephen was sitting on the wall outside the house. Looking back, he was in a terrible place. He was just sitting there on the wall. And he carried my dad's coffin. He insisted on doing that, even with his shoulder the way it was."

Stephen kept a low profile at the funeral, but he joined the family for a drink at the *Red Lion* in Cheadle after the ceremony, where he informed everyone that he had moved into a flat on the Lancashire Hill estate in Stockport.

During the wake, Stephen started talking with a lady he had not seen since he was a child: Alweena Awan, Joanne's former housemate from college whose bed Stephen had slept in during his visits with Mary and Mike. Alweena had trained as an educational consultant and owned her own holistic therapy practice in West Yorkshire.

"Alweena knew Stephen's story," said Joanne. "She knew that he'd become an addict. She was one of my closest friends. They had a good talk after the funeral. They connected straight away. I said, 'Stephen, this is Alweena', and that was it for about an hour or so. They were just locked in conversation."

Alweena remembers the conversation well.

"Even though it had been years since I'd last seen him, I've always felt I've known him," she said. "We had a soul connection. He was very special – I had never met anybody with so much energy."

This meeting would prove to be an important one. Alweena and Stephen would later develop a strong spiritual relationship. It would, however, be several months until they spent time together as mentor and student.

After assuring his family that he would stay in touch and inviting them to his place, Stephen slipped away at around 10:00 pm, leaving the Redings to wonder when they would see him next.

§

The Lancashire Hill housing estate is a high-density housing project in Stockport that was developed in the late-1960s. Located half a mile north of Stockport town centre, this large, 10-acre site consists of four low-rise housing units – Stonemill Terrace, The Bentleys, The Longsons, and Clarkethorne Terrace – that sit in the shadow of two 22-storey tower blocks, the Hanover and Pendlebury Towers, which can be seen from miles around.

Lancashire Hill has little in the way of local amenities, and the utilitarian architecture makes this a somewhat uninviting place from the outside. The area has unfortunately become associated with deprivation, and the actions of a few have resulted in the estate having a poor reputation when it comes to crime. However, Lancashire Hill is home to a diverse group of residents, from families and younger occupants to the older homeowners who have lived there since the estate first opened.

While negative media reports can unfairly malign one's perception of an otherwise ordinary neighbourhood, we do know of one criminal who resided in Lancashire Hill during 2004: Stephen Reding, who was not only happy to have secured his new apartment but was also thrilled at the prospect of being so close to the shops in the town centre, where his fortune was waiting.

From his flat at The Longsons, Stephen could easily access Stockport via the main road that led directly to Prince's Street. Far more appealing, however, was another route – one which took him around the back of the housing estate, down Penny Lane, and along a path that wound its way under the M60 motorway. After skirting the unkempt edgelands along Fred Perry Way, the traveller would find himself slap-bang in the middle of town. It was the perfect rat run for the modern-day *grafter*.

If Stephen had previously exhibited reckless behaviour, he was now pressing the self-destruct button for all it was worth. Wrapped in heroin's sweet embrace, he started to risk anything for the next hit. Of course, the pawn shops didn't accept bottles of spirits as a down payment, so Paul introduced him to the men and women who plied their illicit wares in the local pubs or from the back of their van; the fences who glide silently through every town across the land, furnishing their customers with all manner of tax-free goods. These morally dubious middlemen became Stephen's lifeline as he looked for new ways to fund his habit. He had joined Greater Manchester's hidden underground network of worker bees – and he was good at it, too. Flying on all cylinders, each day presented a new challenge and fresh excitement. These are the professions of an English opium-seeker: stealing booze, clothes, electronics, and cosmetics. Everything was fair game.

Little is known of Paul and Jester, the two individuals who featured in Stephen's handwritten list of lenders. It is known that Paul was older, more experienced, and Stephen's go-to man for drug connections. Meanwhile, Stephen offered no stories involving the mysterious Jester, although it is thought that they were both of a similar age. Despite the lack of any further details, the three became close in 2004. Paul and Jester essentially moved in with Stephen not long after he obtained the keys to his place. His flat on the third floor of The Longsons became the disorderly band of brothers' unofficial HQ, a base from which they planned their schemes.

Despite having a readymade studio space in his flat on Lancashire Hill, art took a back seat for Stephen during this time. There are no paintings or sketches tied to this period in his life. It seemed that all he wanted to do was get numb. Yet although he wasn't painting, Stephen never stopped being creative; it was just that now his creativity was being applied to other areas of interest, mainly how to get cash as quickly and easily as possible. As he had shown when emotionally shoehorning money from his family, Stephen could be a ruthless opportunist, a master of deception, someone who could look a person straight in the eye and in that same moment steal products from the shelf.

Stephen's good looks may have assisted him as he mastered the role of confidence trickster, but by now the signs of his addiction were clear for everyone to see. His hair was shorn close to his scalp, which only seemed to amplify the gauntness in his face and the hollowness around his eyes. He had stopped looking after his teeth, which on close inspection had not been cleaned for weeks. And even in the summer heat, long-sleeved tops were *de rigueur* – not for fashion reasons, of course, but out of the necessity to hide the track marks.

It's not known whether Stephen had any seizures during this time, but he continued to shun his epilepsy tablets in favour of a different type of medication.

"I was living in Leeds," said Ian. "He used to go missing. You wouldn't hear from him for weeks, and then eventually he would call. But when he got his own place, I kept coming over to see him. He was speedballing and all sorts. I mean, with his epilepsy on top of that, his body was just fucked, absolutely fucked. I tried my best to help, but you can't help somebody on heroin. They have to help themselves. It's really difficult. Others had to go through much worse with him than me."

§

The three amigos had a good thing going for a while, but this run of good fortune wouldn't last forever. Whether it was his suspicion-raising appearance or just plain bad luck, Stephen was eventually caught stealing from a department store in Stockport.

"He said to me that *Marks & Spencer* was his lifeline for money because he'd go in and take a hundred pounds worth of spirits every day," said

Victoria. "He said he knew where all the cameras were and that he would just confidently put his rucksack on the floor and put a few bottles in. But they caught him. When he told me about it years later, he did an impression of this 'old biddy', in his words, walking along – you know, with the faces that he did. Well, it was this old biddy that went to the security guard, and that's when he got caught."

Stephen was apprehended and thrown into the security room that was reserved for the store's most undistinguished guests. The police were on their way.

True to form, Stephen managed to talk his way out of the situation. Perhaps he put on the waterworks, or maybe he just stayed silent. Either way, the store manager decided against pressing charges, instead offering a final warning for him never to return.

Stephen was escorted out of the store by a police officer, PC Moore. As they walked out into the shopping plaza, he took Stephen to one side and spoke to him. He hadn't seen this young man before and, in what would become a shining example of community police work, sought honestly to ensure that he got back on the straight and narrow.

"He ended up meeting this policeman on more than one occasion," said Victoria. "Stephen said PC Moore always said to him, 'You don't look like a typical thief. What are you playing at?' That kind of thing."

Of course, the one occasion Stephen got caught was a drop in the ocean compared with the number of times he'd gotten away with the goods. But this was still a pivotal event. With Stockport's retail hotspot out of the picture, the IOUs started to add up. Stephen and Paul were becoming an annoyance to the local dealers, always promising reimbursement before vanishing from the face of the earth. Prior to being apprehended, the daily scams were barely enough to cover Stephen's habit. Now that his face was known, a vital revenue stream was under threat. It was time to take a breather. He had to cast the net wider.

He turned to a couple who had thus far fallen under his radar.

"He came to visit, and we could tell that he was on something," said Stephen's grandmother, Kath. "We had gone for a walk, and when we came back, he was crouched inside the little porch at the front of the house. And he was obviously having a fix of some kind. You know, he was kneeling with his arm out."

"Hi, Nana. Hi, Grandpa. Can I come in?"

A bleary-eyed Stephen sweet-talked his grandparents over tea and biscuits. And when he left, one of their chequebooks went with him. He was just one faked signature away from £400. *Cha-Ching.*

Kath and Roy were furious when they found out what had happened. Roy, in particular, took great offence to the theft, and it would be many months until the two would reconcile.

§

At one with the city in all its guises, it was here that Stephen mastered the art of How to Disappear Completely. He traversed the open fields, followed the brooks and streams in silence, and took the shadow routes from street to street. He mooched his way past the Seven Arches under the cover of night, moon-tanned and in search of a place to sleep. He stared darkness in the face and gave three cheers to oblivion. Oh, how beautiful this dystopia could be.

Mary remained steadfast in her approach towards her son. She did, after all, have a house full of children to look after and a home to run. Not long after her father's funeral, she travelled with Becky to drop off the remainder of Stephen's belongings at his flat. He didn't invite them inside. Although it was comforting at least to know where her son was living, the situation was still emotionally painful.

"It's the one thing that makes me sad," she said. "Because I lost contact with him. I went for months without speaking to him. I thought, 'What have I done?' I prayed so hard about it. I just felt that unless he wanted to help himself, I couldn't help him. He did occasionally contact Victoria to let her know that he was okay. And I had given him the message that when he was ready for my help, I would be there. But it still didn't sit right with me."

§

Aaron "Whitey" Whitethorn[8] was a mid-level drug dealer from the Stockport area. He lived in a modern, terraced house on a quiet street that was connected to a playing field via a passageway. Beyond the field was Reddish Vale, a large country park that follows the path of the River Tame. The banks are often steep as the river snakes its way impatiently down to Stockport, where it joins the Goyt to form the Mersey just a mile downstream. A wide path follows the route of the old Stockport–Denton railway line. This path leads to the main entrance of the park, where the visitor is greeted with an unobstructed view of the impressive Stockport Viaduct. A large black and gold statue marks the route of the Trans Pennine Trail. At the base of the waypoint, there is a poem:

> Down a wandering path
> I have travelled,
> Where the setting sun
> Lies upon the ground,
> The tracks are hard and dry
> Smoothened with
> The weather's wear,
> My mind did move
> With them that had
> Before me been,
> Trodding down the ground
> A track for me to follow,
> Leaving marks for others
> A sign for them to follow[9]

- David Dudgeon, 1999

Offset from the main thoroughfare, which remains popular among walkers and cyclists, a network of unmarked paths connects the Lancashire Hill estate with other areas to the north and east of Stockport. And it was here, on one fateful summer's afternoon, that Stephen and Paul set off to score.

Whitethorn answered the door, and the pair entered the house, which was well-kept and nicely furnished. Stephen had never met the dealer before; Paul had only recently acquired his number through an acquaintance. As the three men walked through the hallway and into the kitchen, Stephen caught a glimpse inside the living room. A young lady approached with a baby in her arms. She closed the door on the imminent transaction.

Stephen and Paul left the house and decided to walk back to The Longsons via the same route. They slipped down the tree-lined alleyway and out onto the field. The sun was beating down as they made their way across the grass. The heroin was already weighing heavy in their pockets. They couldn't wait to sample the goods. Although Stephen's flat was less than two miles away, they decided to get high right there and then. Under a clear blue sky, they sat down and set up along the field's perimeter.

From opium fields to inner city playing fields, this is the way the narcotics flow. A butterfly flapped its wings and a rush of euphoria coursed through Stephen's body. At that moment, they were the blissed-out kings of the vale.

After staring up at the heavens for what seemed like an eternity, Stephen's life would be forever changed through the utterance of one simple sentence:

"Listen, Ste, I've been thinking. There's no way Whitey keeps all his shit in that house."

"What do you mean?"

"There's no way he keeps his stash there, not with his missus and his kid there. If the flat got raided by the police, it'd be too much for him to say it was for personal use."

"You think?"

"I'm serious. If I were him, I'd stash it in this field. Look, you can see his bedroom window right over there."

Stephen cast his eyes across the field. Paul had a point.

Whether it was a drug-induced flight of fantasy or a momentary flash of inspiration, within seconds the pair were scrabbling in the undergrowth, looking for a sign.

Considering there was a huge area along the fringes of the field where someone could hide their contraband, Paul and Stephen had set about trying to find a needle in a haystack. But once the idea had entered their minds, they were determined to leave no stone unturned. They staggered around like ostriches in the ferns.

Astonishingly, they didn't have to search for long. Just a few minutes into their twisted treasure hunt, the stars aligned. Paul kicked over half a brick and saw that the ground underneath had been disturbed. He brushed away the soil and found what looked to be an old army tin. He opened it, slowly. They had hit the jackpot – the mother lode.

"Mate!" he whispered, excitedly. "Come and look at this."

Stephen's eyes lit up.

"Holy shit."

After examining the goods and nearly falling over with delight, Paul took a glance over his shoulder before stashing the container in his battered old rucksack. He placed the brick back over the hole and tried to cover it with some weeds.

Without hesitation, the pair hurried off out of sight, whooping like hyenas as they crossed the River Tame and disappeared into the grizzly maze.

Untitled 56 (2005)
Pen and ink

CHAPTER SIXTEEN

Low

A BLACKED-OUT MERCEDES pulled up to The Bentleys, the long six-storey housing block that forms the backbone of the Lancashire Hill estate. At the heart of the development, a large central courtyard and car park, Kings Court, is pressed between The Bentleys and its parallel unit, Stonemill Terrace. The view to the south is dominated by the imposing Hanover and Pendlebury Towers – those twin high-rise monoliths of emerald green and enamel white. You can almost hear the silence from the 22nd floor, high above the industrial arteries, the commercial veins. The B6167, A626, M60. This could be anywhere.

To the west, Lancashire Hill faces a small industrial district that accommodates a range of businesses: auto parts and gearbox sales, floor surface supplies, audio equipment hire, wedding services, and refrigeration chemicals. *The Navigation* pub sits atop the hill, perched on the edge of a busy, five-pronged roundabout.

The area's most prominent feature, the confluence of the River Tame and the River Goyt to form the River Mersey, has long since been hidden from view. The source of this iconic river is now obscured by a motorway bridge, with the young waterway enjoying just one hundred metres of open air before being culverted, unceremoniously, beneath the *Merseyway Shopping Centre*.

Of course, the intricacies of the landscape mattered little to the occupants of the fast German car. For that evening, as the four lads cruised down Lancashire Hill and turned left onto Penny Lane, it was clear that they were after just one thing: street justice.

§

Stephen squinted through the peephole of the door and breathed a quick sigh of relief when he saw it was only Jester. He pulled his friend inside by the collar, took a cautious glance up and down the corridor, and closed the door swiftly behind him. The brass knocker tapped against the weight of the slamming door. Inside, the blue smoke that filled the apartment had been stirred. A vortex separated into slow-moving fingers.

"What the fuck, man?" said Jester, as he readjusted his shirt. "I've just had a car full of meatheads ask me if I'd seen you two."

"Fuck. Where?"

"Just down the road. They're circling the estate."

Jester walked into the living room to find Paul sprawled across the sofa. The place was a mess. The coffee table was littered with drug paraphernalia, there were overflowing ashtrays, empty beer cans, and cider bottles everywhere. The green army storage tin had been tossed into the corner of the room. It was empty.

"What did they say?" Stephen asked.

"Shit, is that all that's left?" Jester's attention had shifted from the empty tin to the scraps that remained on the table.

"Yeah, it's gone," said Paul. "We sold some though."

Stephen pulled the curtain aside and peered through the window. Things were getting heavy.

"Fuck me."

"Don't worry, we've got a bit of cash, and everyone's going to pay us back," said Paul.

"Why would I be bothered about that?" said Jester. "I've got £20 here. I need a hit."

§

Stephen later told me how, after having taken a stealthy look at the contents of the tin right there in the field on that fateful day, the pair hurried back to his flat. Upon closer inspection, they realised the haul was even bigger than they had initially expected.

—It was *this* big.

Stephen cupped his hands together to create a sphere that looked to be roughly the size of a tennis ball.

—There was this much heroin and a load of uncut coke.

My cousin failed to mention the potential value of the drugs when he recounted this story to me. Years later, in lieu of any concrete figures and working only with his body language as a guide, I carried out a highly unscientific experiment that I hoped might at least give an indication of what the goods were worth: I cut open a tennis ball and filled it with flour, to represent the heroin. I found that half a tennis ball holds approximately 25 grams of flour, so a tennis ball-sized amount of heroin weighs something in the region of 50 grams. In today's figures, a wrap of heroin – around 0.1 grams – sells for £10, or £100 per gram. These figures give Stephen and Paul's haul a potential street value of £5,000. When we include the other drugs that were stolen, they could have easily been sitting on more than £6,000 worth of contraband. Admittedly, this is far from cartel-level shipments, but it was enough for the pair to realise that they needed to do more than keep one eye over their shoulders. There was no way a cache like this would go amiss.

At this stage, the reader might ask exactly why the pair chose to run off with the drugs there and then. It would surely have been much wiser to at least have waited until the dead of night – or better yet, several days – to reduce any suspicions that tied their presence in the area to the missing heroin. But their hunger for the H outweighed any such reasoning.

This decision would transpire to be a poor one. Stephen didn't realise that behind his softly spoken exterior, Whitethorn was a power-hungry dealer who wouldn't think twice about putting someone in hospital for misusing his trust. This attack on his enterprise – the theft of his main stash – was immeasurably worse. Now the word was out, and Stephen had every right to be worried.

§

After discovering the drugs on that sublime summer's day, Stephen and Paul started to formulate a plan. They knew they had to distance themselves from the drugs as quickly as possible. They quickly concluded that selling most of the heroin would be the best course of action. Before doing so, however, they decided it would be rude not to sample the wares and dream about all the things they were going to do with their imminent windfall. Of course, reality did not match their expectations. The discovery of the heroin opened the doors to a drug binge of bacchanalian proportions. Stephen's flat became a popup trap house, as people came over to party – day after day, night after night. *Golden brown, texture like sun.* Of the countless windows in every direction, how many were hiding secrets of their own? *Lays me down, with my mind she runs.* The wind blows hard; the wind blows cold. *Throughout the night, no need to fight.* Sensing the ripples that pulse through space and time. *Never a frown with golden brown.*

As the days turned into weeks of unbridled heroin use, one may wonder if Stephen ever thought about getting clean. Did he ever catch a glimpse of himself in the bathroom mirror, with the music pounding through the door, and question what he was doing? Or was he just so deep into the drugs – deep in the throes of that never-ending high – that the thought of getting clean never even crossed his mind?

§

Jester had been with the pair of fugitives every step of the way, but he still couldn't believe the stash was gone. Stephen's flat told the tale of a sordid affair, subjecting the visitor to sudden, gruesome flashbacks. Chaos was organising itself around them. The *Cenobites* were coming.

By this point, Stephen and Paul knew all too well what would happen if they were caught by the dealer and his boys. The retribution would be swift and harsh.

"So, what did they say to you?" Stephen asked as Jester found a place to sit among the clutter.

"They asked if I knew anyone called Paul and that he'd been hanging out with another lad in glasses."

"Fuck."

"I don't think they know exactly where you live, though, because they were down at the main car park."

"What? Really?" Stephen turned to Paul.

"They're looking in the wrong place!" they both said in unison.

As the northernmost of the six Lancashire Hill housing blocks, The Longsons has its own parking area, Cymbal Court. The fact that Whitey and his boys were camped out at Kings Court, by The Bentleys, gave the pair a little respite. But the dealer was determined, and if sitting in a car park on a tipoff was the best they had, then so be it.

The heavy mob was a worry, but Jester's comments had made them all realise they had an even bigger issue: Where *were* they going to get their next hit? They were almost out. All other avenues of enquiry had been exhausted. The sharks were circling outside, and it would not be long before the pain of withdrawal started to set in.

Devoid of any other sources of income, Stephen and Paul used what little money they had from selling their ill-gotten heroin to buy even more drugs. In fear of venturing outside, they used Jester as their inconspicuous errand boy. But eventually, that money ran out as well, leaving Stephen and Paul with no other choice but to resume their day-to-day routine of petty theft and low-level scams.

§

Christmas came and went, and 2005 arrived with no sign of Whitethorn or his boys. In retrospect, it's remarkable that Stephen and Paul were not accosted in the days and weeks after the stash was stolen. The dealer threw a ring of steel around the area. But no one snitched.

The dust might have settled, but Stephen was still more cautious than ever. Not only did he now have to keep his wits about him when targeting retailers, but he also had to stay alert when out on the streets. To make matters worse, since finding the stash Stephen's tolerance for opiates had increased greatly. In the end, it was perhaps inevitable that his luck would run out.

One cold February afternoon, Stephen was caught attempting to steal some display items from the *Index* store in the *Merseyway*. The police were called, and Stephen was eventually joined in the security room, once again, by PC Moore – the dyed-in-the-wool beat cop who had let him off with a warning following the *Marks & Spencer* incident just weeks earlier. This time, however, the authorities would not go so easy on him, particularly as a security guard had caught a cuff to the head in the fray, immediately adding assault to the list of charges.

Stephen was taken to the police station and placed in a holding cell. After being interviewed, he was informed that his case would be taken to Stockport Magistrates' Court, where he would be charged. Pending his court date, he was banned from entering Stockport town centre.

§

Stephen and Paul had come out of the woodwork and had suffered no repercussions for their actions. They might have got away with it, too. The only problem was that the pair still owed money to all the local dealers, and they were once again in dire need of a hookup. A malevolent force was brewing, and the withdrawals were now really starting to hurt.

A month after he had been apprehended in *Index*, Stephen and Paul made a decision that was perhaps even more foolish than stealing the drugs in the first place, as they turned to their only remaining contact: Aaron Whitethorn.

"That's it, then," Paul said to Stephen as they were lounging in The Longsons. "We should call Whitey and pick up from him."

"You *what?*"

"Yeah, we should call him."

"Are you fucking mental?"

"What? We've not seen or heard from him for months. He doesn't know it's us. If anything, it would seem weird if we *didn't* go around anymore.

"You reckon?"

"Yeah, man! Come on, use my phone." Paul threw his battered *Nokia* in Stephen's direction. Stephen caught it and sat upright.

"What? I'm not bloody doing it."

"Yeah, go on. He doesn't really know you. Just say I've been in hospital or something."

"But I thought you said you—"

"Just *call* him, mate."

The pair soon realised that the dealer's suspicions would be raised if Stephen were to call him from Paul's phone. Instead, they walked out to the phone box in Kings Court. Paul cast a hopeful glance towards his accomplice, as he quietly composed himself and picked up the receiver.

§

"Alright, mate, yeah… Okay, cool. See you soon."

Stephen hung up.

"Well, what did he say?"

"He said to meet him on the field near his house in half an hour and that I can pick up from there."

"Oh, right. You'd best set off, then."

"But why would he ask to meet me there? You normally go inside his house, don't you?"

"I only went there once or twice before. His missus has probably got some friends over or something."

After some discussion, Paul and Stephen parted ways.

Less than 20 minutes later, Stephen crossed the bridge over the River Tame and half-jogged up the hill towards the meeting place in the corner of the field – the very same field in which they had found the dealer's stash.

He approached the meeting point, pulled up his collar, and discreetly cast his eyes to the exact spot where they had found the haul. As he arrived, three men slowly fanned out from the alleyway, followed by Whitey.

"Alright, pal? Where's Paul?"

"Paul? I don't know, ma—"

Something flashed in the corner of Stephen's eye. He turned just in time to see a large wooden object flying towards his face. The cricket bat connected with a sharp wooden crack – *Bap!*

One of the assailants rifled through Stephen's pockets. And they were gone.

Stephen floundered on the ground as the sound of screeching tyres echoed down the road.

The Hostel, Part I (2005)
Ballpoint pen

CHAPTER SEVENTEEN

Memories of the Future

STEPHEN TAPPED HIS LIGHTER on the table. My mouth was ajar.

—I'm sorry, James.

He sat back in his chair and knocked the foam from his beer. His voice was tense, excited.

—I'm sorry. I just wanted to tell someone.

After all those months of uncertainty, Stephen's candidness was refreshing. It was almost as though once he started talking, the floodgates opened. His eyes widened as the words came tumbling out of his mouth. He was reliving those times as he spoke, each passing syllable turning his memories into something concrete, tangible.

I urged him to continue.

The only reason he was still alive, Stephen said, was because the dealer thought that Paul was the mastermind behind the theft. His reasoning? The angle of the weapon during the attack.

—They were looking for Paul, but when they saw he wasn't there, they used me to send a message to him. They hit me with the flat side of the cricket bat. If it had been the sharp side, I might have been dead.

Warning short or not, the beating was brutal. After lying there half-conscious in the mud on that chilly February evening, Stephen mustered enough strength to pull himself into the dense patch of trees and undergrowth that lined the south side of the field. And there he stayed, alone and utterly defeated.

§

It is plausible that the dealer believed Stephen was nothing more than an unwitting accomplice to the theft, which took place in that very same field just metres away from where he now lay. But while the beating could have been much worse, the cricket bat incident had deep repercussions. This latest mugging was just one of numerous attacks and altercations that Stephen fell victim to throughout his life, but at that moment, as he clutched his head and cried under the stars, he decided to get clean.

Stephen spent the next two nights on that field. He couldn't bring himself to go back to his flat at The Longsons, not after everything that had happened. He had taken the role of a drug addict to breaking point. He had to get out of that world. This was rock bottom. This madness had to end.

That he slept rough in winter with no money or shelter is enough alone to demonstrate the impact the beating had on him. Whitey no doubt would have moved his stash spot following the theft, but Stephen's decision to remain there at the scene of the crime, under threat of the gang returning at any point, goes a long way to describe his mental state. A sprinkling of good fortune had come his way in that it was an unusually mild February.

As he lay there with his head pounding and in the throes of withdrawal, did he recognise the bitter similarities between this latest beating and the mugging that resulted in his epilepsy more than a decade earlier? Of course, the key difference between the two incidents is that while Stephen was a truly innocent victim in the first incident, this fresh assault was a revenge attack that many would consider inevitable, if not wholly justified. After all, the street has its own code from which no one is exempt.

It's impossible to know exactly what went through Stephen's mind that made him choose to hunker down in that field, but it was clear that it was preferable to what lingered behind the door of his flat. He was at a crossroads in his life, and he was unwilling to go back. He was tired of the lies, the stealing, and the constant hustle to acquire drugs.

§

Dawn broke on the second morning, and Stephen finally mustered the strength to head back. He cautiously walked down the corridor to his apartment, placed his ear to the door, and turned the key. Once inside, he was greeted by an aroma of stale smoke. Stephen peered into the lounge to see Paul and Jester nodding out in the armchair and on the sofa. He saw the remnants of the night before on the table. They had obviously found another plug. A crushing feeling of temptation flashed through his mind, but he turned and continued his silent mission, moving quickly into the bedroom, grabbing a rucksack, and filling it with a few possessions before moving into the bathroom to do the same. He left without making a sound.

Stephen checked himself into a shelter and day centre for homeless and vulnerable people in Manchester city centre. The staff there patched him up, gave him some food, and assigned him a sleeping pod.

It's not known how long Stephen stayed in the shelter, but the change in environment gave him the headspace to decide what he was going to do next. The people he encountered there – the volunteers, the social workers, and indeed the other residents – gave him guidance and lent him a non-judgemental set of ears. He decided he would attend counselling sessions and focus on his recovery.

The administrators at the centre referred Stephen to another non-profit in the centre of Stockport that supported those who were homeless or at risk of losing their homes. Here, Stephen was introduced to Nicholas Warner, a community drugs liaison officer who had been assigned to help support his recovery. He was a caseworker, a counsellor, and a key part of Stephen's support system. He assisted him with cancelling his lease at the flat and started the ball rolling for alternative accommodation.

During his time in the shelter, as Stephen's body slowly adjusted to an environment without heroin, he received a call from Ian. Although the two friends had never lost touch, they had not been speaking as regularly as they used to – not since the drugs started to take hold of Stephen's life. However, this well-timed phone call would be another pivotal moment in his ongoing recovery. Ian was keen to understand what had caused his friend to travel down such a dangerous path. He had tried to help Stephen get clean before, with little success. But things were different now. Stephen was finally making a change.

By the time the call had ended, Stephen had a plan.

"I took him to Leeds," said Ian. "Josh had a house, and I used to rent a room from him. Ste came to live with us there. He was getting himself clean, so I said, 'Come and live with us in Leeds!' And he did."

Stephen's decision to move across the Pennines and to a new city would prove to be a positive one. He was able to distance himself from the community in which he had found himself, or perhaps helped create. There was too much weighing down on him in Stockport. He needed more space.

"We were trying to get him in a different environment where he was out of all that," said Ian. "Where he didn't have those contacts. Just to give him a completely different head change."

It would be comforting to say that Stephen made a swift and direct recovery, but this was not entirely the case; his emergence from that terrible period of chaos was not always smooth. Ian noted that Stephen would still go missing from time to time, and it is thought that he may have occasionally slipped back into his old habits.

"We were trying to get him a job and get him sorted out, and he got mugged at one point," said Ian. "He got robbed in Leeds. I don't know really what happened. It always seemed a bit suspicious. He said that some lads offered him a lift back to the house, and he got into the car. Apparently, they just robbed him and beat him up. I couldn't quite understand it. It was strange because it was during the day. He'd been out shopping and had bought some clothes and art stuff. He was in a really good headspace, and then that happened and it really knocked him back. It just seemed odd though, I couldn't understand why. It just seemed strange that someone would offer you a lift, that you'd get in the car, and then get mugged like that."

Fortunately, incidents such as this were little more than minor road bumps in Stephen's ongoing recovery. When it came to finding employment, however, things proved to be difficult. With all other job leads coming up short, Stephen started to sell *The Big Issue*, mainly in areas where his face was not known.

"One of our friends saw him selling *The Big Issue* in Guiseley, which is a bit further out from Leeds," said Ian. "He'd obviously taken to doing that, and we didn't know about it."

It's not clear whether Stephen neglected to tell his friends about the position out of embarrassment (not that he would need to; *The Big Issue* is a fine publication and a true force for good), or if he simply wanted to focus on getting himself together without anyone else's input. Either way, his actions go a long way to showing how determined he was to take charge of his life and get himself back on track.

This was a difficult but revitalising time for Stephen. And although there were still plenty of hurdles to overcome, he was feeling much better about himself.

After a few weeks in the room at Josh's house, Stephen moved into a new place nearby. "My mate Sam had a spare room at his house, just around the corner from me," said Ian. "Ste moved in there. He now had a proper room and was paying rent."

In April, Ian drove Stephen back to The Longsons one last time. The rental contract had ended. Paul and Jester were long gone. Stephen collected the rest of his belongings, left the keys on the kitchen counter, and never looked back.

§

Back home in Cheadle, the Redings had no idea of the changes that were going on in Stephen's life. Although Stephen had briefly informed Victoria that he was no longer living in Stockport, the family had precious little information to go off. Mary's concerns were further raised during a church gathering in June:

"I was at a birthday party one Friday night, and a friend came up to me and said, 'Oh Mary, I'm so sorry. Have you not seen this week's *Stockport Express*?' She'd seen the listings in the newspaper. Stephen had been to court. Stealing. And he'd been done for it."

When she returned home, Mary dug the free newspaper out from the recycling bin and found a short entry on page four, in the weekly 'In the Dock' section. A snippet from the list of court cases read:

STEPHEN JOSEPH RED-ING, 29, of The Longsons, Lancashire Hill, has been convicted of assault and stealing two drill sets worth £63.98 from Index in Merseyway. He was conditionally discharged for 12 months and ordered to pay £25 compensation.[10]

Mary took the news of Stephen's arrest away with her to Lourdes, as she embarked on her annual pilgrimage. Although she had laid out clear boundaries the last time she had spoken to Stephen, this latest revelation caused her to rethink her approach.

"I remember going to Lourdes and praying so hard about it," Mary said. "I thought, 'What have I done? I've cut my ties with him'. I had told him, 'If you're not happy to have the help I can give you, then I can't do any more for you'. But it didn't sit right with me, and I thought, 'No, I've got to give him unconditional support. I don't have to give him any money'. I came to the conclusion that maybe what I felt was the right kind of help for him might actually not be the right kind of help because I didn't know what his needs really were. So, I came back from Lourdes, and I said to Victoria, 'I need to see him and speak to him. Next time he calls you, get him to phone me'."

During that time, in the summer of 2005, neither Victoria nor Mary would know when Stephen would next be in touch. However, just two days after his mother's return from France, he called Victoria to inform her that he had been assaulted in Stockport and was heading to the police station. Victoria urged him to call Mary.

Another assault? Their thoughts were running wild.

"I spoke to him for the first time in months," said Mary. "He called me from the police station, and he said he'd been clobbered, again. I said, 'Wait there, I'll come and meet you and we can talk'. So, I drove to Stockport and met him at the police station."

Mary hurried into the police station to find Stephen sitting in the waiting room. Given the circumstances, she may well have been expecting to find her son at another low point in his life. It soon became clear, however, that this wasn't the case. The court case Mary had read about involved an incident that took place months ago. Stephen was already in the process of getting clean.

"He told me that he'd been seeing a counsellor and that he was getting all the right kind of help he needed," she said. "He said he was no longer taking heroin and that some lads had mugged him for his methadone prescription."

Woman with Third Eye (2004)
Oil pastel, pen and ink

CHAPTER EIGHTEEN

Back to Life

"HE'D BEEN ASSAULTED – well, battered – quite badly," Mary explained. "I don't know whether these people knew he was no longer using, or if it was someone who had a grudge against him. You know, Stephen had lost quite a few friends and had made a few enemies in his day. But one thing I do know is that he was really upset about it. He had been trying so hard to work on his recovery, and then he got battered again. He phoned Victoria and she just said, 'Phone Mum'. She felt that he needed me and that it was right that he phoned me. I was able to meet him and talk to him. And we never looked back. He went from strength to strength after that. He never used after that."

As disheartened as he was for having been attacked once again, this incident played an instrumental role in Stephen's recovery. It resulted in him reuniting with his mother, and soon thereafter the rest of his family.

At the height of his drug-taking, Stephen tried his best to become an island. After being marooned for so long, it took him a little time to fully reconnect with everyone. However, following their rendezvous in the police station in August 2005, Mary started to meet up regularly with her son. They would often grab a coffee in Stockport after he'd met with Nicholas, his counsellor. Although he was still residing in Leeds, Stephen continued to work with Nicholas, with whom he had struck up a productive relationship, and travelled back to Greater Manchester at least once a week.

"Nicholas was amazing," said Mary. "My original message to Stephen, a while ago, was, 'When you're ready for my kind of help, let me know'. In fact, he wasn't looking for my kind of help – he'd already sought all the right help. What he really needed was family love and support, which we had for him. But he was already on the right track. And he never came off it. He was incredibly strong and incredibly brave."

Although she was initially cautious, Mary and Stephen soon rekindled their relationship. And with this, the patchwork sheets of the family network gradually started to stitch back into place.

"When Stephen was on drugs it was unbearable," said Chris. "But it wasn't Stephen. When I first saw him clean, it took me a long time to adjust. But we went to *The George* for a pint, to talk it over. And it was really good. You could see that he was coming back to himself. As I said, it was horrible to live with and horrible to see, but on the upside, the most beautiful thing was seeing him recover."

For Andrew, too, the change in his brother was profound. "He didn't really even have to make amends with me," he said. "When he was coming clean, I remember saying to him, 'Anything you owe me, Ste, just forget about it. The slate's wiped clean'. I know what it's like when you're in debt. I guess I did keep him at arm's length at first because we used to meet up somewhere for a coffee. He wouldn't come to me. After a few weeks, he said, 'Andy, can I borrow £20?' And I just said, 'Sure, here you go'. And two weeks later he gave it back to me. It was such a change, and he was only six months into the treatment."

The treatment Andrew mentioned was methadone, a synthetic opioid that is sometimes used to treat chronic pain but is much more commonly associated with its use in opiate maintenance therapy. For the past 50 years, the drug has been used to treat heroin addiction and opioid use disorders. Taken most commonly as an oral solution, methadone can help alleviate some of the symptoms of opiate withdrawal. It is administered in controlled doses that taper down over a period of 12 months or more. In theory, this allows the affected individual to quit heroin with as few side effects as possible.

In the UK, methadone is used in a state-run drug rehabilitation programme. Patients can be placed on the programme after receiving a doctor's prescription, and usually need to visit a pharmacist or other licensed distributor centre every day to receive their methadone dose.

On paper, methadone appears to be a good solution to a difficult problem, but this approach is not without its detractors. Make no mistake, methadone is a powerful and addictive drug in its own right. Some studies indicate that instead of becoming opiate-free, some users in maintenance programmes can succumb to dual addiction as they supplement their daily methadone dosage with illegally obtained heroin or opiates. In the same stroke, there is a growing trend for abstinence-based programmes. Dovetailing with the argument that methadone does nothing more than substitute one drug for another, this method encourages total forbearance of harmful substances, focusing instead on the user's spiritual recovery and development. On the other side of the debate, many studies have indicated that methadone and similar drugs can be successful. The *Royal Pharmaceutical Society* supports it as a valid treatment. In addition to the physical relief a patient can feel when they ingest the drug, another key aspect of any opiate maintenance programme is that it can help the user break away from any social groups or environmental triggers that might otherwise increase the likelihood of them using.

Stephen retained a copy of *The Methadone Handbook* – a 23-page booklet he received during his initial consultation, where he was taken through the treatment. "Prescribed methadone can provide a useful period of getting used to life without heroin before becoming drug-free," the booklet reads. "Being stable in treatment can be the basis on which people start to build a way of life away from heroin use."

It is beyond the purview of this book to advocate for any one method of treatment. It is likely that different approaches work better for different people. For Stephen, however, methadone helped. It gave him the structure in his life that he needed, allowed him to break free from certain social circles and provided a safety net for the worst of the withdrawals.

§

Despite his ongoing success in his battle against heroin, Stephen's attempt to secure a job in Leeds continued to be a fruitless exercise. No doubt his criminal record and lack of experience impacted his ability to find employment. His self-esteem was at a low ebb. He was unsure what to do with his life now that he was clean. A huge question mark seemed to hang over everything.

It was at this juncture, as Stephen navigated his way through the stormy and emotional waters of recovery, that he finally returned to his long-lost passion: art.

As can be seen in the letters they sent back and forth on their various travels, Ian and Stephen always had an artistic connection. Ian was now a professional photographer, and he encouraged his friend to start painting again.

"I was really pushing him with his art," said Ian. "And he started to paint again. He sold a few to some friends in Leeds."

In addition to working on bigger and bolder pieces, Stephen came up with the idea to turn some of his paintings into greeting cards and postcards and sell them in packs. He designed a business card, which read:

Ste Reding
Artist/designer

§

Among the many small but significant events that each marked a step in Stephen's recovery throughout 2005, the christening of Victoria's son, Shaun, on September 3rd stands out as a highlight. Though they were now living in Salford, the ceremony would take place in Cheadle, followed by a barbecue at the Reding house.

It was a glorious late summer's day, and the extended family all joined the celebration. Although Stephen had previously been in touch with most of the people there, it would be the first time everyone was together at the same time. It would also be the first time he would meet his Nana Kath and Grandpa Roy since he made off with their chequebook some eight months ago. He was understandably nervous, but despite the pressure of the situation, Stephen was front and centre at the ceremony.

Even before the first hymn had rung out, he showed that he was still partial to a joke. As the congregation lined up at the gates of the church, Stephen's cousin, Lauren, introduced him to her partner (and future husband), Patrick Kennedy.

"It was the first time he'd seen a lot of the family since everything that had gone on," Lauren said. "We were all standing outside the church. I said, 'Ste, this is Pat'. And Ste, straight-faced, said to him, 'I heard you're seeing my cousin. You'd better not mess her about'. And then he just walked off. Pat didn't know what to think. But Ste just turned around and said, 'I'm only messing, mate. How's it going?' It was hilarious."

"I remember everything he was wearing that day," said Stephen's brother, John. "He had a shaved head, he wore sunglasses all day, and he was wearing a dark grey and black striped top, blue jeans, and smart white Fila trainers. And I remember, it felt like he was sad that day. It seemed to me the reason he was sad was that he felt like he'd let everyone down. It was almost overwhelming for him, with everyone being there. But there's a picture of the whole family in the back garden. It's a brilliant photo."

Despite his initial reservations, Stephen soon realised that his worries were unfounded. Everyone was just happy to have him back.

"I remember him being so happy, once he realised that everything was fine," said Lauren. "I just went up and gave him a big hug. It was a great day. We played basketball and football. He had his top off at one point. I remember his tattoo."

Of course, among the party members were Kath and Roy Reding. "That was the first time he saw nana and grandpa," said Lauren. "It was one of the reasons he was so nervous." However, Stephen and his elders put the past behind them. Smiles filled the garden as everybody saw him talking and laughing with his nana and grandpa, just like he used to.

"It was wonderful that he was back," Kath said.

"That day was a turning point," said Chris. "I remember him saying, 'What a great day'. No one was in his face. He said he knew he still owed us money, but we all just said, 'Don't worry about it, just focus on getting your life back on track'."

"The day is still looked upon as my favourite," said David, who was so moved by the occasion that he committed his thoughts to paper in a journal entry:

How Stephen made the recovery, or when, is to my mind unclear. What I do know is that on this day he was well and truly back among us. The whole family was there. It was a gloriously hot day.

I'll never forget an incident that took place after Mass but before the guests arrived. Mum, Stephen, and I were in the garden preparing the seats. He approached her and asked if he would be welcomed at the party. I was on the other side of the garden. He was 29 years old, yet his body language was more akin to a 10-year-old's. In that fragile moment, I saw my brother for what he was: a good, kind-natured man who had been driven through the depths of despair and stripped of his charming arrogance and pride. He was scared stiff, and I know he might have preferred to be anywhere else on that day. To my mind, the best quality a person can possess is humility, but it is one that many people rarely find. Seeing him in that glaring sunlight, he laid his soul open and let his demons surface. He felt unworthy to be there – but if only he could see what I saw. I was prouder than I have ever been of anyone in my entire life. I just wanted to hug him. The need to do that was taken away by my mother. She looked at him and reassured him that everyone was proud of him and that all we wanted was for him to be happy.

I remember one quote from that exchange. Stephen said, 'How do I face them, Mum?'. She said, 'With your head held high. This moment was always going to happen, and it is up to you to show them how far you have come. You have nothing to hide and everything to be proud of'.

There was an emotional hug between the two. It was palpable. Love is rarely expressed so tangibly. You could almost touch it. His spirit was ignited, and he faced the crowd. His confidence was destroyed, his esteem all but diminished, but he walked around the crowd that day and spoke honestly and frankly to everyone. He must have been terrified, but looking at him you wouldn't have known it.

After witnessing that conversation with Mum, I kept a close watch on him. And he was the Stephen of old. I remember we were both talking with Uncle Peter, with a beer in our hand and sufficiently tipsy. We were talking about something and nothing, and then we shared a look with each other that touched my heart. It was a carefree look from Stephen, as though to say, 'What was I worried about?'

Stephen was back. Although the road would be long, he had emerged from the quagmire. The battle had been won, but to maintain peace takes a different type of mettle. He would need the love of those around him and a strength of mind that could defeat anything. I look back on this day as the time when he realised that he had both.

§

Shaun's christening certainly marked a turning point for Stephen. It was such a contrast to previous family events, such as Uncle Ced's visit when he was monosyllabic, or David's 18th birthday party when he dropped the needle. But of course, none of this needed to be mentioned. The smile on Stephen's face said all that needed to be said. It was a great party that ran well into the evening.

As the sun sailed down to the horizon and the barbecue flames began to fade, Stephen caught my attention and asked me if I wanted to play a game of chess.

We set up the chessboard on a small table in the back garden, opposite the side entrance of the house. People were coming and going. I had recently come back from travelling, and so we swapped stories about Thailand as he smoked his rollups. He told me he used to play lots of chess when he was in Thailand. And it showed. He won both games.

As we wrapped up the game, I mentioned that I was working on an album and asked if he would like to get involved in the design of the CD cover. He enthusiastically agreed, and we said we would meet up when the project was nearly complete.

§

Although Leeds had proved to be one of the best decisions Stephen had ever made, at the end of 2005 he decided it was time to move on. As Ian recalls, his friend's lack of success when it came to finding employment played no small role in his decision.

"He tried his hardest to sort himself out and get a job in Leeds, but it just didn't work for him," said Ian. "He just couldn't get a job. He was trying and had some interviews, but it just didn't happen. If he had managed to get a job then things would have probably got going, but it didn't and it just got him really frustrated and almost stagnated."

Yorkshire had been a sanctuary for Stephen. It was a place for him to regroup. But now, following the buoyant family reunion in September, he finally had the strength to return to Manchester.

Aided by his counsellor, Stephen submitted a housing application to Stockport Council and was placed on a waiting list for accommodation in the area. In the interim period, he continued to spend an increasing amount of time with his family.

As Christmas came around, Stephen volunteered to help find a pub that would become the venue for the Reding and Walker families' Christmas lunch. After making enquiries, Stephen and Lauren settled on *The Junction* in Cheadle Hulme.

"He was delighted because he had been around all the pubs," Mary recalled. "We went to *The Junction* because he found out he knew the chef. But when Christmas Day came around, he was worried because he thought, 'What if nobody likes it?' He was the one who chose it. But we all loved it."

With the family gathered merrily around the table, the moment marked a stark contrast to the Christmas just a few years earlier when Stephen was missing in Thailand. This difference was felt no more than by the man himself. He sat there with a smile on his face through all three courses before heading around into the side room to watch *The Snowman* with the younger ones by the fire.

Later that evening, Stephen informed his mother that he had been offered sheltered accommodation in a house in Edgeley, just outside of Stockport town centre.

"In all that time he went from strength to strength," said Mary. "They don't give these places out to just anyone. They only give them to people who are on the road to recovery. It's a bit like a halfway house – it's for people to have a chance to get back into society. They have people to help them. The one thing I feel sad about is that there were times when I was very suspicious, and wrongly so. Stephen used to reassure me. He said, 'I'm never going back. I know it's hard for you to believe, but I'm never going back'. And that Christmas I really knew he meant it."

Study for Alweena (2006)
Oil Paint on Canvas

CHAPTER NINETEEN
Infinitum

For Manchester is the place where people do things.
'Don't talk about what you are going to do – do it.'
That is the Manchester habit.[11]

- Judge Parry (1912)

IN THE TWELVE months leading up to our meeting on March 11th, 2006, Stephen had been pushing ahead with quiet determination. He had been free from heroin for nearly a year and had a fresh outlook on life. All things considered, he was becoming himself again, and just breathing it all in.

That final hit was a literal and metaphorical smack around the face. That cricket bat became a lightning rod for change. Despite all the beatings he received at the hands of others, my cousin's biggest war was the one he fought with himself. The process of recovery was not an easy one. It forced him to be vulnerable and open himself up to his emotions. But now, after having lived for so long in that self-imposed exile, he was bouncing back stronger than ever before.

I grabbed my jacket and my rucksack and headed for the door. Like everyone else in the family, I would be there with him every step of the way.

§

A letter confirms the date that Stephen moved into his new accommodation:

Housing Benefits Department
Stockport MBC
Piccadilly Street
Stockport

<u>Landlord's confirmation – Notice of Rent</u>

Dear Ms [Redacted],

Please acknowledge this letter confirming that Stephen Reding moved into a property at:

Aberdeen Crescent
Edgeley
Stockport
SK3 9EJ

On 9th January 2006

The total rent payable is £118.67 p/w.

Yours sincerely,

Project staff: [Redacted]

A stone's throw from Stockport town centre, the property was managed by a local housing association that provided support for vulnerable people, including recovering drug addicts and victims of domestic abuse. The house featured four bedsit-style rooms, each with a sink, kitchenette area, and locking doors. There was a shared toilet and bathroom upstairs, and another toilet downstairs. Also on the ground floor was a large, shared kitchen and communal living room.

It might not have been the fanciest of places, but the house on Aberdeen Crescent provided Stephen with a solid foundation. The term 'halfway house' is no longer widely used, but if this simply refers to a place that's halfway between where you came from and where you want to be, it may well have been appropriate in his case. Ultimately, it was a springboard from which he could launch himself back into the world.

As part of his supported housing, Stephen had been assigned a caseworker, Sara Simon, who was on hand to assist him with his job searches and other responsibilities, as well as being the sounding board for any issues in the house. Stephen attended weekly 'Linkwork' sessions where he could discuss his recovery and any challenges he was facing.

Both Sara and Nicholas, his counsellor, assisted Stephen with his finances, and his debts were consolidated into one amount. Sure, he would be paying it off for a long time, but the monthly fee was manageable. His obligations were clear and attainable. He was finally regaining control. And what's more, Stephen now had the freedom to pursue his art with no restriction.

Even before he had moved into his new flat, Stephen was painting at an intense rate. He was in the midst of a fervent period of creativity, producing increasingly bold and abstract pieces. As can be seen throughout the pages of this book, Stephen was adaptable to many mediums – including ballpoint pen, and even his own blood. But if anything, he worked best with paint.

With little in the way of disposable income, Stephen found it difficult to afford the canvases that were for sale in the art shops. Instead, he took to lining his frames with discarded material or cut-up old curtains. This small detail goes a long way to demonstrating the strength of his creative impulses during this time. As small as his flat was, it was here that Stephen produced some of his best artwork. He returned to Stockport armed with nothing but a desire to paint. And it was precisely when he moved back to his hometown that his art started to take off as a modest commercial venture.

After taking cues from those around him, Stephen printed off his first batch of greetings cards.

"He wanted to start doing the gift card thing," said John. "Ian had taken pictures of his artwork, and I was helping him format them on the computer. He was printing them on photo-quality paper. And it was great to have him back. I know it's a bit of a cliché, but it's true. He asked me if I knew anyone who could set up a website. So, he was really trying to get things off the ground."

The cards were simple but impressive. Others liked them, too. The first letter to arrive at Stephen's new address was from his Auntie Joanne: "The cards are really superb, and I can't wait for the day to get you to come and do paintings all over my home," she said. "I hope the link with Alweena was good – she just loved them and was astounded at your talent."

The link that Joanne refers to was a potential commission. Stephen's aunt had previously shown Alweena some of his paintings, and she expressed the desire to purchase a piece of artwork from him.

Other letters praising Stephen's artwork came, but it was this project for Alweena that marked the start of what he believed to be a promising new venture. Although he had painted for friends and acquaintances in the past, this was his first official commission. What's more, after discussing the painting with Alweena over the phone, he found out that it was destined to take pride of place in her clinic.

"For some reason or another, he wanted this to be so right for her," Joanne said. "They had both discussed the picture. They had had their own private conversation, and he found the right energy to do it."

Such was the importance of this commission that Stephen put himself under a great deal of pressure to deliver his best possible work. Unfortunately, his first attempt ended in disaster.

"The painting that hangs in my living room picture was originally for Alweena," said Victoria. "He rang me in absolute tears because he ripped the canvas. He'd already finished the painting. He called me earlier that day and said, 'I finished it! I finished it!' But then, a couple of hours later, he called me to say there was a hole in it. He'd knocked it over and it had ripped. He was devastated. In his eyes, he had to redo the whole thing. Normally he'd use old curtains for his canvas, but for this one, he used proper artistic material."

Despite this initial setback, on Thursday, February 9th, 2006, Stephen boarded a train to Bingley with a painting under his arm.

For Alweena, it was worth the wait. Stephen gently cut through the paper packaging and presented her with a striking oil painting.

"It's a painting that heals," Alweena said. "Of course, all his pictures tell a story. If you look at the one that he painted for me, this one is light. I have it in my consultation room. It's a very healing picture. When I have kids in the clinic, they just look at it and look at it. Children are absolutely fascinated by it. There is so much in that painting, it shifts into a different dimension. Just like music can be healing or how some people can be healers, this is a healing picture. He was a healer. He could connect with something greater."

Alweena added: "I remember picking Stephen up from the train station. I wanted to show him that he could make a living from his art and that it was worthwhile. I just had an intuition that he never believed in himself. That was the big problem: he never really believed in his own power, and that's why he diverged. I had long conversations with him. We spoke on the phone. I said, 'Well, you know you could actually be painting'. I wanted to buy a painting to show him it was doable, commercially. When I first saw his cards, I thought, 'Wow, that's really amazing'. Those little cards of his were just so simple but so profound. That day, he talked to me about how scared he was to bring the painting to me. He never felt worthy of his own work. He didn't realise how good he really was."

Alweena didn't typically work with male clients at her clinic, but given her decades-strong ties to the Reding and Workman families, she made an exception. On the day that he gave her the painting, she conducted a spiritual balance on Stephen.

"We talked and talked and talked – for a long time, maybe two or three hours," Alweena recalled. "And I said, 'I'd like to do a session for you'. We talked about his epilepsy. One of his biggest disappointments was not being able to drive. In some ways, I think he associated that with a lack of freedom. But he was moving on from all of that. Regardless of his artistic talent, his greatest gift was self-forgiveness. It's the hardest thing to do in the world, to forgive yourself – but by the time the session had ended, he was so peaceful. He said he would stop blaming himself and judging himself or worrying about whether others forgave him. He came to this huge self-forgiveness."

Stephen took the train from Bingley to Leeds and then another train back to Manchester. How happy he must have felt, as he cut through the snow-topped hills, knowing that he'd made his first proper commission and was a step closer to finding peace.

§

The sun shone down over Manchester as I rode the bus into Stockport. From Rusholme and Fallowfield to Withington and Didsbury, Parrs Wood and the Heatons, down into the valley.

I met Stephen outside the War Memorial Art Gallery. He was sitting on the steps, underneath the numbers etched into stone: 1939—1945. A smile snapped across his face when he saw me crossing the road.

It was the first time I had met my cousin, alone, since everything that had gone on. It felt great to be with him, as we walked down Greek Street to his place on Aberdeen Crescent, full of conversation.

He opened the door, and as we headed upstairs, he pointed out the living room - a good-sized space with a red carpet and mismatched furniture. Once we were inside his room, I saw just how seriously he was taking his art. His flat was more like an artist's studio with a bed. There were paint tubes and canvases strewn all around; paintbrushes and easels soaking in the sink; sketches and paintings everywhere. With windows to the south and east, the place was flooded with natural light. It was a beautifully chaotic space.

Several complete canvases were laid up against the wall. In the centre of the room was the painting he had been working on for the album I had recently finished recording with a friend [see *Prologue* image]. I walked right over to it.

—Wow!

—It's nearly there. Can you see the treble clefs in it?

—It's perfect. Honestly, it's amazing.

—Well, get your camera out and we can always take more pictures once I've finished it.

We spoke about many things as we sat there on his bed, drinking cups of tea. He offered me some advice on a relationship that was falling apart. We talked about music and his art. I encouraged him to approach some bars and cafés in Manchester, with a view to showcasing his work there.

As I cast my eyes around the room, I saw a photograph of a topless young woman lying on a beach. Stephen saw where my eyes had landed.

—She was the one it all started with. Emma.

This was the first time Stephen had discussed Emma, or his hard drug use, with me since his return. But once he uttered her name, he proceeded to tell me everything, from his descent into addiction to his emergence on the other side.

Stephen's painting would feature on the CD of the album I had been working on.[12] I had other ideas for the cover image: a location in Cheadle. After sharing this with Stephen, we decided to complete the project that very afternoon. Given that it was such a nice day, we decided to go for a drink first.

My cousin had his sunglasses on and a spring in his step. As we neared the bus stop, by the bowling green on Edgeley Road, our conversation turned to methadone. Stephen informed me that he was down to 20ml per day and would soon be off it completely.

—So, what… what is it?

—It's a liquid that you take once a day. It's not heroin, but if you drank it, you would be seriously ill.

—Don't worry, I'm not going to try and drink it.

We boarded the bus. It was so busy that we had to sit apart. We were silent as we travelled down to Cheadle, passing the site on Bird Hall Lane where 15 years earlier Stephen had epilepsy thrust down upon him through that senseless assault.

He deftly rolled a cigarette in his lap and turned and smiled as we got up to leave.

§

Throughout early 2006, Stephen spent time with everyone in his family. Their recollections indicate that he had come a long way in his recovery.

Chris saw how passionate his brother was becoming towards his art. "The best moments with Stephen were when he was painting," he said. "It was hell when it was me, Andy, and Ste in that room for six months – absolute hell. But now it was different. Andy and I lived not too far away from Ste. I remember when he went to Mum's house to paint the picture that's in her living room now. He just put the canvas up on the wall and would go around and work on it every day. I was there sometimes, and it was mesmerising to watch him. It's huge. It took him a while. But you could see in his face… you could see he was back. We'd got him back."

In addition to his art, Stephen developed a newfound love for the local football team, Stockport County FC. He lived a stone's throw from the stadium, Edgeley Park, and would sell programmes on match day, taking a small commission for each purchase and watching the game for free. His brother Andrew was a lifelong fan, and one day they decided to go to a match together, along with Andrew's partner, Heather. It was clear that Stephen wasn't taking the game too seriously.

"There was this chant, *Chrissy Turner's blue and white army!*" said Andrew, referring to the former club manager. "But Heather and Ste started their own chant. I just remember them singing, at full volume, 'Chrissy Turner's blowing Tommy!'"

Andrew recalled another occasion when he was standing in the garden with his brother. In awe, Stephen said, "Look up! God, how clear it is to see the stars!"

"He was looking up to the sky and turned back down and gave me a big thumbs up," said Andrew. "He was just looking up in amazement."

On the other side of the family, with amends now made, Stephen would often visit his grandparents, Kath and Roy.

"He started coming over quite regularly," said Kath. "We talked about family history, and we talked a lot about the war. He used to come and sit with a smile on his face. He was quite content."

For Irene and Geoff, the other dear septuagenarians in Stephen's life, the change in him was clear to see.

"Stephen had a tough time," Geoff said. "But he came back. He was rehabilitating. He was on his way. One particular night, it was a Saturday night, he came to visit, and it seemed like we talked all night."

Stephen's cousin Lauren recalls him being keen to share his newfound love for reading.

"He was always trying to get me to read," she said. "*The Da Vinci Code, Nineteen Eighty-Four.* I also remember going to the pub with him one evening. He was nervous because he thought he was going to bump into an ex-girlfriend. I spilt a drink on him. He was really worked up about it because he was worried about seeing her. He was in the toilets with his shirt under the hand dryer. I felt terrible."

Although Stephen once again embraced his role as big brother, the occasional argument is still known to have taken place. But all things considered, these day-to-day clashes of character may simply be an indication that things were getting back to normal.

"We were either really close or we argued like cats and dogs," his sister Becky explained. "There was one time that we didn't speak to each other for a good week. If Stephen was at the house and one of us walked into a room, the other walked out. We ended up having a huge argument. I can't even remember what caused it, but we were saying anything we could think of to make our arguments better. I think he called me a spoiled brat, and I was crying hysterically. But the next time he saw me he gave me a homemade card that said, 'I'm sorry for all the things I said. You're growing up to be a really lovely lady'. And he said, 'If you ever need a hug or someone to talk to, I'm there'. That card means so much to me."

Of all the mended relationships, the one between Stephen and his mother perhaps stands out the most. The two would meet regularly, and it was not long before they were laughing, joking, and talking like they used to.

"When Stephen was ready to come back, he did so to wide open arms," Mary said. "He was rebuilding all his bridges, but the biggest gift was that he started to love himself again. You could see that peace in his eyes. He was at peace. He was incredibly strong and incredibly brave."

Mary knew that her son was riding the wave of a prolific creative streak. And although she encouraged his artistic pursuits, she also voiced her concerns about his health. She urged him to take care of himself, particularly after he said that he was often staying up well into the night to paint.

"He told me he'd had a couple of seizures," Mary explained. "I remember once going into his flat and saying, 'Stephen, it stinks of turps in here!' And he said, 'Hmm, yes, perhaps I should open the window. It's just a bit cold'. And I said, 'It's probably these fumes that are making you have these bad seizures'. He said he was taking care of himself, that he was taking his medication, and not to worry."

Stephen was indeed taking care of himself, in many aspects of his life: He had a busy social calendar and had created a basic fitness and nutrition plan. Although he still drank alcohol and would occasionally smoke cannabis, hard drugs had long been out of the picture. Stephen, however, strayed from the truth when he told Mary that he was keeping up with his epilepsy medication. He had not taken any since March of the previous year.

Notwithstanding these pharmaceutical falsehoods, Stephen confided in Mary and often discussed his plans with her.

"He hoped to become a counsellor himself, like Nicholas," Mary said. "I think it was partly that he didn't want anybody else to make the same mistakes. I guess you could say, 'Well, what kind of example did he set?' But the things that happened to him, he so desperately didn't want them to happen to anybody else."

One afternoon in early 2006, Mary and Stephen were out together in Stockport. As they casually browsed their way through *Marks & Spencer*, Stephen turned to his mother with a mischievous look in his eye.

"I'm still banned from here, you know. I just wanted to see if they recognised me."

The security guards and staff at the department store could easily be forgiven for not recognising the young man, who just 18 months earlier had been caught red-handed. He was a different person now.

The change in Stephen was evident on another occasion in Stockport, when he and his sister Victoria bumped into PC Moore, the policeman who had tried to steer him on the right path all those months ago.

"PC Moore said, 'Oh, you look really well'," said Victoria. "They had a little chat. Ste said what he was doing, that he had started doing some paintings for people, and he told him where he was living. PC Moore seemed happy to see him. He said, jokingly, 'You're not getting yourself into trouble now, are you?'. As we walked away, Stephen said to me, 'He was dying to check my bag'. But I didn't get that impression. To me, he seemed genuinely happy that he was getting his life in order."

There are many more accounts that highlight the great strides Stephen had taken during his recovery, but there is no clearer indication of his positive outlook than in two letters he wrote during this time.

The first was addressed to Ian. Stephen wanted to thank his friend for everything he had done:

Hey Ian,

How are you doing, my old friend?

So you are a wee bit more informed… I am doing very well – I don't think I have had a better state of mind. Don't do drugs. Very rarely drink alcohol. Up at 7:00 am every morning. An absolute want for filling my head with knowledge, skills, nature, the trees… basic life and love, the things that are very easily forgotten about when one is caught up in the rat race (whatever the rat you're running with is up to).

I am truly sorry for the times I have failed. You are an amazing friend. Stuck by through thick and thin. You should be very proud… and I am sure you are let down also. As am I, my friend. I know I have fucked up… for some of those things I am very ashamed. I used to tear my head apart in protest and frustration. 'I can't deal with this, face up to all this. It's too much of a mountain to climb'. I would become depressed and self-destruct, which ultimately led back to my addiction.

I am also very proud of you – goes without saying. But also of myself, Ian. I have certainly not forgotten, but I have allowed myself to move on. It was the only way to conquer – to put everything right and to achieve all my goals and dreams.

It tastes different, Ian. Young again, but wiser, cooler, and happier.

I love you, Ian x

These themes of admission and self-forgiveness continue in another letter written by Stephen, which is made all the more powerful when it becomes apparent that it was addressed to no one but himself:

How have I gotten into such a huge mess?

How have I managed to let so many people down?

For each of you whom I have let down mean the world to me.

Why, then, have I failed you? Why have I failed myself?

There is absolutely no excuse for the way that I have behaved, and no one else is to blame other than myself.

All I will say is that I was driven by something so strong that I still find it hard to comprehend.

I am so ashamed of myself, and I am truly sorry.

I had tried to combat this problem of mine before. After a short time, the doorways of my mind were once again open. All those troubled thoughts and emotions that had been suppressed for so long came flooding back.

Everybody had been so kind and more than understanding, but I had made a tremendous mess of everything and had let so many down that I was finding it increasingly difficult. I absolutely hated myself.

Unfortunately, this ultimately led back to the problem I had initially fought so hard against, which in turn would create a whole new set of problems.

I was in the centre of a vicious circle. Again, I only had myself to blame.

I have faced my demon once again, only this time to be a complete success.

I have had to put all the mess I had created to one side.

I have by no means dismissed or forgotten about any of the wrongdoings for which I am responsible.

I am afraid that – apart from apologising for my mistakes and providing starting to put all the correct pieces back into place – it may take some time, certainly longer than I would like, for me to repay everything in full.

I am so very sorry for everything.

§

The residents of the house on Aberdeen Crescent generally kept themselves to themselves. But after taking Mary's advice regarding the fumes and ventilation, Stephen had taken to painting downstairs in the communal living room. And with this room being adjacent to the front door, he quickly became acquainted with the other housemates.

"He was painting anywhere," said Mary. "He was painting downstairs, and he was encouraging all the residents to use the sitting room. The lady from the housing association said he was a role model for the residents."

During his time at the property, Stephen found a friend in Akram Aziz, a young, quietly spoken Iraqi man who lived at Flat 2. Though Akram didn't drink alcohol, Stephen would take him out to the pubs around Stockport, and he once took him to the local nightclub.

"The man at the door told Stephen to take off his cap before we could go inside," Akram said. "As soon as we were inside, he put the cap back on his head. He was a very funny man."

In addition to going to the pub with his siblings who were of drinking age, Stephen spent a great deal of time with his youngest brother, Jamie. In the space of a year, he went from absent brother to having a friendship with his nine-year-old sibling that was stronger than ever, as he escorted him to school and other activities, often making a quick detour via the local sweet shop.

§

We sat there in silence, as the glasses clinked and the people talked. Time had gone full circle.

—Come on, we'd best get going.

We placed our empty glasses at the end of the bar and left through the stained-glass doors, making our way merrily towards St Mary's Church.

After walking through the tree-lined entrance, we looked up at the spire. *TIME IS FLYING.*

Stephen took a picture of the eastern clock face at precisely 4:18 pm:

I asked him if he thought the image looked right, aesthetically, with the hour and minute hands being so close together. He was amused at my fastidiousness.

—I think it looks great.

We walked out of the churchyard, back down the high street, and stopped at the World War II monument, our parting place. I invited Stephen to a party I was hosting the following weekend, which he said he would try to attend.

We hugged and said our goodbyes. Stephen walked off in the direction of Cheadle Heath, and I headed north towards Manchester. With the artwork for my project complete and my cousin back in the frame, I was feeling good.

§

In his letter to Ian, Stephen confessed his newfound passion for knowledge and enlightenment. For his aunt Joanne, Stephen's artwork tied all these strands of intellectual enquiry together.

"He had a beautiful portfolio," said Joanne. "When he came to visit the previous year, it was a lovely sunny day and we sat in the garden and went through all his paintings. He spoke about all his inspiration for them. He was peaking."

Joanne added: "We shared a similar language. He wanted to understand himself better. He wanted to know his evolution and his reasons for being here and where he was going. And he kept a very open mind about it all. He didn't judge anything or anyone."

After spending time with Stephen during his last visit, Joanne caught up with her nephew again during her next trip to Manchester – an occasion she remembers well.

"The 25th of March 2006 was Peter's birthday," she said. "It was such a beautiful day. We all met at Mary's house, and Uncle Geoff, Stephen, and I decided that we would walk to the place we were eating lunch in Cheadle Hulme. That walk was so bizarre. It was like we walked the journey of

Stephen's life. And we all swapped stories throughout the journey. First, there were magpies, and Stephen said, 'I keep seeing magpies everywhere, what do you think that means?' And he told me about Alweena, that he'd met up with her and was going back to see her. He said that she'd helped and that he really felt at peace with himself."

Joanne added: "On the journey, we came to a bridge. And as we were standing on the bridge, we were looking down the stream, and it looked familiar to me. And then we realised that this was the back of his nana and grandpa's house. You know, the Micker Brook near Crosseffield Road. And I said, 'I can see you and your dad in that river now'. I remember sitting, years ago, on the side of the bank and Stephen was hanging off a tree branch over the stream. Mike was going to catch him when he let go. I could see Victoria and Andrew there as little toddlers. And on that walk, we spoke about many things. He wasn't troubled by anything. There was no 'poor me'. He was at peace. He was enjoying his life.

Joanne continues her account of the day: "We went into the restaurant, and I was sat next to Stephen. I said, 'By the way, how did you get on with your book? How did you get on with your journal?' We weren't doing Christmas presents that year, but for some reason, I just saw this Leonardo Da Vinci journal in the charity shop. Something just attracted me to it. And I bought it, for £1.50 or something. And I thought, 'Who am I going to give this to?' And the next time I saw Stephen, he said to me, 'I want to write a book'. So, I gave it to him. It's a beautiful journal, with the *Vitruvian Man* and all those famous sketches and paintings. Back in the pub, I said, 'How's the writing going?' And Stephen said he hadn't started writing yet'. As of the 25th of March, he had not written in that journal at all. I said, 'Don't think about it, just write anything, write the words that come into your head. Don't worry about the English, don't worry about the scrawl – just get words down on paper'. And he said that he was going to."

Late afternoon dissolved into the evening, and after another leisurely walk back to Mary's house, the family ended up going out to eat yet again – this time at the local Chinese.

"We went for *another* meal!" said Joanne. "We had an early lunch then went out again. It was just hilarious by this point, totally crazy. I was laughing so much that they couldn't tell me to stop. We went back to Mary's again, and Stephen said he had a late Christmas present for me. It was one of his paintings, and it was just lovely. And my last conversation with Stephen that evening was when he was getting ready to leave. And I was desperate for the loo. I can just remember the feeling of that moment. He said, 'Auntie, I've got to go now'. I said, 'I'm dying for the loo, just wait'. He said, 'No, I'll just get on now'. And we kissed and hugged. I said, 'Thank you so much for my gorgeous picture. Now don't forget the book'. And he said, 'I'm going to come up and see you soon anyway'. And I said, 'Stephen, *mi casa es su casa*'. He was at the door, and I just blew a kiss, and then he left."

§

On Friday, March 17th, I received a call from Stephen. It was the day before my party.

—Hey, Ste, how's it going?

—Great, thanks. Listen, I know you have this party tomorrow. I'm really sorry, but I'm not going to be able to make it. The thing is, I've met someone.

I was a little disappointed, as I wanted to introduce my cousin to my friends. But there was something in his voice. I could tell he was looking forward to his date. He was almost giddy with excitement.

I wished him good luck and said I looked forward to hearing all about it next time we met.

§

Saturday came around, and before he went to meet his date, Stephen went to visit Mary.

"Mum and I had been shopping," said Becky. "I'd just bought my first ever mobile phone and was excited to unbox it. He was excited about his date – we were both excited!"

Little is known about Stephen's new potential love interest, but according to Mary, he was very keen on her.

Becky added: "It was about to rain, so Mum said, 'Here's an umbrella, and you might as well take a bottle of wine, too'."

Stephen strode out to meet his date, dodging the puddles with the bottle of wine and umbrella in tow. Though he felt a mixture of nervousness and excitement, he was grounded in the present moment and ready to embrace whatever life brought his way.

Untitled 16 (2001)
Acrylic paint, ballpoint pen

The Tide Will Sway

ON THE EVENING of Monday, April 10th, 2006, Greater Manchester Emergency Services received a frantic phone call from Akram Aziz. His words tumbled out to the operator on the other end of the line.

"H–hello? Please, we need an ambulance to come to Aberdeen Crescent in Edgeley. It's urgent."

Less than 10 minutes after the call, at approximately 10:45 pm, paramedic Jonathan Butterworth entered the property and was guided up the stairs, where he found the lifeless body of Stephen Reding slumped by the side of his bed.

He was 30 years old.

Self-portrait in a Hand Mirror (2006)
Chalk pastel, charcoal pencil

CHAPTER TWENTY-ONE

After Image

THE HOUSE PHONE RANG the following morning. Mary's partner Charlie answered the call.

Mary was working at the reception desk at a local medical centre.

"Charlie – what are you doing here?" she asked, as he walked through the door.

"Mary, I've had a phone call. It's the police. They want you to make a private call and head home with me."

The police car pulled up to Mary's house at around 11:00 am. Detective inspector Dominic Winters and detective sergeant Stuart Fairchild walked down the garden path.

"Mary Reding? Can we come in?"

§

The news of Stephen's death hit his family like a freight train. It sent a shockwave through the Reding household. The discovery of his body had set the wheels in motion for a flurry of activity, starting first with the ambulance services who had descended on the epicentre of the incident, followed by the police, and then through the hearts of those he was closest to.

Stephen's brother Chris was one of the first to be informed.

"I'd been out in Manchester the night before with all my mates," he recalled. "The phone rang at about 11:00 am. I never used to answer the house phone because it was always junk calls, but something made me think, 'You need to answer this', so I answered it. *Hi, Chris… it's your mum.* I just knew something was wrong. She said, 'Stephen's passed'. I said, 'What do you mean, he's passed?' She said he'd been found dead. I blurted out, 'Please don't tell me it's drugs'. Tears started pouring down my face. I was in a meltdown. I couldn't believe I kept it together, but Mum didn't know what to do and we knew everyone needed to be told, so I told them to come to mine and we could start making some calls."

Three hundred miles away, in Scotland, Joanne was waiting in line to order a cappuccino in a café in the Spittal of Glenshee. "I was travelling up north with a friend," she said. "It was bizarre because the week before, I had been saying, 'I'm so unsettled, I can't focus on anything. I feel strange and I don't know what it is'. Mary called me at noon to say, 'Where are you?' I said I was just standing there. She asked me if I was driving. I said no."

"Joanne. Stephen's dead."

She ran back to the car and made a beeline for Manchester.

During her brief conversation with Joanne, Mary was reminded that her son John would soon be returning home after a weekend in Perth. Before setting off for the Cairngorms, Joanne had dropped John off at the train station.

"I put him on the eight o'clock train, so when I heard the news, I knew that John was still on the train. And I couldn't bear it. I couldn't bear the thought of him on that journey, not knowing anything."

"Mum, Charlie, Andy, and Heather eventually drove back to Mum's house to meet John," said Chris. "I followed in a taxi about half an hour later. Andy called Victoria at work, and she came straight away, and so did my dad."

"I was at a friend's house in Gatley," said Becky. "My mum called their house phone and said, 'Tell Becky that she needs to come home. Charlie is on his way to come and pick her up'. At that point, I knew something wasn't right. My friend's mum said I had to get ready to leave, but they wouldn't tell us why. Charlie came to pick me up. He was really quiet. I thought it might have been something to do with a family member. We pulled up to the house and went around to the back door and saw lots of people inside the house. I went into the kitchen and some people were crying. And Mum told me it was Stephen. I screamed. I just remember screaming and then crying."

David was staying at his university halls of residence in Sheffield. He was due to return to Stockport in a few days and was confused when Charlie and Chris phoned to say they were on their way to pick him up. "He asked why, but I said we couldn't tell him until we got there," said Chris. "When we saw him, I said, 'Brace yourself, David. Stephen's passed."

§

I knew I was going to be pushed for time during my lunch break, so as soon as the clock struck one, I was out of my office building on Oxford Street in Manchester and on a bus towards Rusholme. I was heading to a print shop in Victoria Park where I had ordered 50 copies of CD label inserts and 50 CD cases. The project was complete. It was the culmination of six months' work, and I wanted to put the final pieces together as soon as they were ready. I had to be back within the hour, and the shop was at least a 15-minute walk from Rusholme. I had no time for food and didn't realise my phone was on silent.

After picking up the goods, I caught another bus back to the city centre. As I walked back into the office, I checked my phone. Eight missed calls.

I guess I also had a gut feeling it was going to be bad news because I delayed calling my mum back for a few moments. I returned to my desk, flustered from the rapid round trip and unsure of what to make of the missed calls. My thoughts were interrupted when the phone rang once again. I answered it in the hallway.

—Mum, what's up?

—Hi, James. Something's happened. I don't know how to tell you. Stephen's dead.

I returned to my desk and sat there for a moment before asking my team lead for a quick chat. As the words fell out of my mouth, I broke down right there on the office floor.

In what lingers as a strange and surreal memory, I boarded another bus and again found myself walking in the sun under the trees to Victoria Park. I was stunned, in a daze. My mum was on her way to collect Lauren from her house. They both picked me up at around 4:00 pm. Before I left, I hurriedly prepared one of the finished CDs and threw it in my bag.

We arrived at the house, which was by this point full of people, including all the Reding siblings and their partners, along with numerous other family members and some close family friends. They were scattered around the kitchen, in the quiet room, in the living room, and in the garden. People were in disbelief and disarray, as they hugged and consoled, and discussed when they last saw Stephen. The atmosphere seemed to shift from near-hysteria to near-silence, back and forth in waves. At the centre of this storm was Mary, who was simply silent. The adults and children all took turns consoling her.

Joanne arrived from her long journey down and took Mary into the bedroom. Years later, she commented on her sister's silent, almost catatonic state.

—It was like she just couldn't take anything in. As a mother, you can't imagine. You just can't go there.

For months afterwards, I remember thinking how uncanny it was that we all gravitated to Mary's house - not knowing why, and not knowing what it would solve. It was magnetic. No matter where people were when they found out Stephen had died, they all headed straight there. It was an automatic reaction. We needed to be together in our grief.

§

The Redings retraced their steps over the previous days and tied this in with what little information they had from the police. Stephen's body had been found on the night of Monday, April 10th, but the first responders could not immediately ascertain the exact date of his death. During the family's discussions, it became apparent that John was the last person in the family to talk to Stephen, on Wednesday, April 5th.

"It was the night before I travelled up to Perth," John said. "I was coming down the stairs and my phone started ringing. I think he'd already tried the house phone. Mum had come back from Scotland that day, so she was already in bed after all that driving."

Mary was keen to hear how Stephen's date had gone and tried to get in touch with him earlier in the week. Her son hadn't answered the phone. According to John, there was no message of any significance to pass on.

"We were just talking," John said. "Mum kind of clung to the fact that I was the last person to speak with him, but he was just calling to say he was fine. It wasn't urgent. He just wanted to speak with Mum, I think for a chat or to arrange a visit the following week."

Mary was open and frank with the detectives and mentioned his history with drugs when they informed her of his death.

"Even at this stage, the police seemed pretty convinced," she said. "They said there was no evidence of anything like that in his room. They said, 'All we know is that there will be an inquest, but there was no evidence of any drug taking'. There were no syringes or other paraphernalia."

The initial appraisal of the scene of Stephen's death went a long way to allaying the family's concerns. There were still so many questions but now was not the time to ask, as the silence was punctured by a harrowing wail that emerged from the living room. It was an unbridled outpouring of grief – an anguished cry from a disconsolate mother.

§

That evening, I was booked to play a gig at a bar in Manchester - an informal album launch, of sorts. I was hesitant to go but decided, with no shortage of earnest sentiment, that it was what Stephen would have wanted.

By this point, at around 8:00 pm, Mary had returned to her silent state. I worked my way into the living room and sat down next to her.

—Hi, Auntie. I'm going to head off now. I brought this for you. I'm so sorry.

I gave her the CD that Stephen and I had made together. She opened the case to see the disc adorned with his artwork before breaking down again.

Untitled 18 (2001)
Pen and ink

CHAPTER TWENTY-TWO

Back in Black

IT WAS ALREADY DARK by the time I left my place in Victoria Park. I set out in the slow rain with my backpack over one shoulder and my suit bag over the other. It was April 20th, 2006 – the night before the funeral. As with almost everything that happened in the immediate aftermath of Stephen's death, I remember that night and the following day with a strange, adrenaline-fuelled clarity.

Given the area's proximity to the heart of central Manchester, the walk from Victoria Park to Rusholme reveals a surprisingly suburban and rather grand neighbourhood. This is the soft face of the city, where villa-style mansions and well-designed newbuilds are set back from the wide, tree-lined boulevards. On evenings such as this, the misty rain diffuses the orange glow of the streetlights on Upper Park Road, transporting the traveller back to a bygone time.

I had walked this route a hundred times. And though the journey always provided a few welcome moments of calm, it was never long before the city reclaimed its hold on one's senses, as the bright lights and busy streets around Wilmslow Road came into view.

§

Due to the unexplained nature of Stephen's death, an inquest had been opened by the authorities. This would involve a post-mortem and his case being brought before a judge, who, after gathering the evidence and hearing any relevant personal statements, would seek to determine the cause.

Once the police had completed their investigation at the scene on Aberdeen Crescent, Stephen's body was taken to Stepping Hill Hospital in Stockport – the hospital where he was born. And there, in a room marked

'Mortuary', he lay in stillness as the wheels of the legal system slowly turned around him.

Mary was informed that Stephen's body would not be released by the coroner until the post-mortem had taken place, and so there were worries that the funeral might not be able to go ahead as planned.

"Mum was hoping for the funeral to be either Friday the 21st or early the following week," said Becky. "It was the end of the Easter holidays – term started on the 24th, and Mum didn't want us to have to go back to school before the funeral had taken place."

Mary eventually received the news that her son would be released in time for a funeral on the Friday. She immediately pushed ahead with the arrangements.

"I remember his body was released, and by then Mum had already planned the entire funeral – the cards, the ceremony, the wake, the gravestone – everything," said Becky. "It all happened so quickly."

§

As I approached Wilmslow Road, I was accosted by two lads who had seen my bags and decided to try their luck. One of them tried to distract me with small talk before the other attempted to swipe my bag from my shoulder. Even under normal circumstances, I wouldn't let anyone get away with my belongings without a fight, but in my highly-strung state of mind, I was filled with rabid energy. The ill-timed attempted robbery prompted a response that was way out of character for me. I pushed them away, confronted them, and screamed like a banshee.

—I'm going to my cousin's FUNERAL! Fuck off!

The lads backed off, whooping curses in my direction as they ran down Denison Road.

Shaken, wound up, and extremely angry, I headed for the bus stop.

§

Everyone in the Reding family reacted to Stephen's death in their own way. Following the initial shock, Mary sprang into action. Perhaps she felt that keeping busy would help prevent her from being taken too deeply into her grief. Others also tried to continue their lives with some sense of normality.

"I went to work the next day," said John. "I know it sounds stupid, but I didn't want to use his death as an excuse. I just felt like I should go in. I was working at the bakers in Cheadle Hulme. I didn't even tell them beforehand. I must have looked terrible. I just told them, 'My brother died yesterday'. They said, 'What are you doing here?' And they sent me straight home. So, I asked my girlfriend to come over and we went to the cinema. I just wanted to do something normal."

"I honestly just remember getting drunk for about four or five days," said Chris. "I remember crying my eyes out when Mum told me. I went back to work on the Saturday. I was there for half an hour, like a zombie. The manager said, 'Just go home. Thanks for coming in, but just go'."

Back at Stephen's flat, representatives from the local housing authority had started the process of sorting out his room. They boxed his belongings and removed the artwork from the walls.

§

The bus finally arrived at Parrs Wood. I set off on foot once again, this time towards Cheadle. I walked down Manchester Road, across the River Mersey, and over the M60 motorway. My pace slowed as I approached Mill Lane Cemetery, where the next day I would be saying goodbye to my cousin for the last time.

§

Just after Easter, Stephen's body was transferred to the chapel of rest at the funeral directors in Cheadle Hulme. Mary went to visit her son as soon as she was told he was there. She was accompanied by her sister Catherine and sister-in-law, Suzanne. Unfortunately, upon their arrival, Mary was informed that she would not be able to see him.

"Normally when you go to a funeral home, they let you view the body, but they wouldn't let her look," said Suzanne. "They wouldn't open the casket because his body was so badly decomposed. No one was able to see him. Mary was distraught when she found out. She was so upset that she couldn't see him one last time."

§

The rain must have continued all night because the streets were still soaked come morning. Mum and I had stayed up late the previous night. Talking, reminiscing - all about Stephen, of course, and the family. There were tears, laughter, and plenty of wine. I showered in a daze, put on my suit, and mentally prepared myself for a day that I knew would be like none before.

The clouds were receding as we drove to Lighthorne Road. At Mary's house, there was a quiet sense of urgency. People buzzed around as they finished getting ready. David was upstairs giving his speech a final read-through. A lone cry of anguish emerged from the living room.

—The car's here.

We all fell silent.

The undertaker, in his black suit and top hat, walked slowly down the centre of the road, followed by three vehicles. There, in the back of the lead vehicle, was the coffin. We came out of the house one by one and gathered round the hearse. Suzanne kissed her fingers and touched them to the car window.

—Oh, Stephen.

We drove in a convoy to the church. Strangers on the street slowed their pace. An elderly man removed his cap in a mark of unexpected reverence.

The family approached St Chad's. A crowd of mourners had already gathered outside. Hugs and soft smiles were exchanged between friends and relatives. An all-encompassing sense of disbelief flashed through my mind, as the coffin bearers were asked to approach the hearse.

The crowd slowly filtered into the church where the scent of wood and candles merged. I was handed a booklet and took my seat on the right. The hall was packed with dozens of familiar faces.

It had not been long since Andrew, Chris, David, and Stephen carried their grandfather Charles through those doors. Now, joined by their father, Mike, they were carrying their oldest brother to the altar. Each step was a struggle, as they inched closer to that incomprehensible conclusion.

The coffin was laid down. Our eyes were downcast as we all waited for the priest to start the service.

The priest was a staunch and unwavering man, and this came across in his eulogy. He spoke directly on issues surrounding addiction, noting that he had acquired a damaging drug habit during his time as a missionary in South America when he was a young member of the cloth. Ultimately, though, this would be a preamble to a celebration of Stephen's life. The theme of the sermon was one of redemption, as the priest highlighted Stephen's continued recovery over the previous 12 months. The light from the stained-glass windows caught the dust motes in the air. I cast my eyes across the funeral booklet as the hymns rang out. Voices rose and then faded to silence. A lady turned around and whispered,

—Peace.

David stood up and approached the altar. He walked up to the lectern, composed himself, and addressed the silent congregation:

So, Stephen is seemingly gone. But he's not. He's just waiting for us to finish the train that is life. He's waiting at a faraway platform that is more commonly known as heaven. So, what are we who are left behind to do? Mourn? Certainly, for a great man has got off this train. Celebrate? Definitely. I can say without any hesitation that Ste would have been severely disappointed if the ones he loved didn't celebrate the miracle that he was. I look around this room and I see many faces. The Stephen that I got to know so well over these past few months would have been incredibly moved by such a fantastic turnout. For I suspect he didn't appreciate how loved he was, how many lives he had affected. But there are a lot of things about himself that he probably didn't know. He never knew how much courage he had. How brave he was. What that man went through doesn't bare thinking about. But he stuck it out and found the strength to dig that little bit deeper.

It is difficult to express the enormity of what Stephen overcame. It is even harder to express how he did it. Or so it would seem. In fact, it is quite easy. He did it for the love of everyone in this room. When times were hard, he thought of all those that cared about him and just ploughed on. These past few months have been some of the best of my life. Why? Because I got my brother back – my cool dude of a brother. That incredible sense of humour, that undeniable wit, that kind, caring selflessness. I, we, got it all back. And we should be proud. Proud for what that man achieved. Proud of who he was. Because I know I am. See you soon, mate.

David gathered the eulogy in his hands, walked back to his seat, and quietly broke down.

In his speech, David talked about Stephen's bravery. The fact that he - a 22-year-old lad - had the courage to stand up there in front of all those people, demonstrates that this was a trait he had also inherited. Now the speech was over, I could see that David let go of everything. That was enough to hit me in my core, leaving only the choir to mask my cries. *And he will raise you up on eagle's wings, bear you in the breath of dawn, make you to shine like the sun, and hold you in the palm of His hand.* Stephen neither expected nor wanted anyone's sympathy - not when he acquired epilepsy nor when he was in the throes of addiction. But at that moment, an overwhelming surge of sympathy is what he got from me. *This is happening. This is really happening.*

Stephen's brothers and Mike were once again beckoned towards the coffin. They carried it slowly down the aisle, followed by the family. I turned to leave and saw that the church was even busier than I'd first thought. There were at least 250 people there, not only filling the pews but also standing around the back and sides of the nave, with yet more people looking through the windowed antechamber and spilling out of the entrance.

At Mill Lane Cemetery, a smaller group of Stephen's family and close friends gathered around a freshly dug plot. A prayer was spoken, and the coffin was lowered into the ground in slow motion. The family each took turns throwing lilies and handfuls of soil onto the wooden casket. Any sense of disbelief slowly washed away, and my eyes blinked at this new reality. The flowers fell without a sound, and our hearts were truly broken.

§

Over the course of the day, we did all the things David urged us to do in his eulogy. We mourned, we celebrated, and we toasted a man whose life had been cut short. The wake was held at Cheadle Social Club, where the mood had thankfully lifted. Stephen's oldest friends, Ian, Josh, Matt, and Jamie, swapped stories around a table. I found a moment to sit down and speak with Akram, Stephen's housemate, and thanked him for those last few months he spent being a friend to my cousin.

As the afternoon drew on, people started making their way to Mary's house. I walked the short distance with David, Andrew, and John, and remember thinking, 'Stephen would just love to be here right now'. We talked and talked, from the afternoon into the evening. We dealt with his death through laughter; the funny stories momentarily helped us forget the pain. *The only person who's missing is Stephen.* I thought back to Shaun's christening - that momentous summer occasion when it was clear that he was back for good.

The one thing that overshadowed the celebrations was uncertainty. Although everyone in the family was confident that drugs hadn't played a role in Stephen's death, there were still so many questions. However, it would be another six months until the inquest, and so for now, the only thing we could do was come together and celebrate Stephen's life.

I didn't want the night to end. I knew it would be the next morning when the feeling of loss would truly take hold.

Ko Phi Phi Don (2000)
Pen and ink, watercolour

CHAPTER TWENTY-THREE

Once Upon a Field

THE MONTHS BETWEEN Stephen's death and the inquest were tough for the family. It was a strange time, a quiet time, an upside-down time. Having to wait for the inquest made it harder to move on.

A couple of days after the funeral, my mum, my sister, and I headed back to Mill Lane Cemetery. Stephen's headstone had been put in place. Etched in white, on polished black granite, his epitaph read:

So Loved,
So Very Loved

†   STEPHEN JOSEPH REDING   †
Aged 30 Years

And He will raise you up on eagles' wings,
bear you on the breath of dawn,
make you to shine like the sun,
and hold you in the palm of his hand

Jesus, remember me
When you come into your Kingdom

I later asked Mary about the words on the gravestone.

—It's a hymn from Isaiah. We sang *On Eagle's Wings* during Stephen's funeral. It's a very moving piece. I thought long and hard about what to put at the top of his grave. Should I put 'Loved Son' or 'Brother' - where do I stop? Those words, 'So Loved, So Very Loved', seemed to cover everybody. But those words came from Stephen. The Christmas before he died, he chipped in for my Christmas present with Becky, John, David, and Jamie. It was Becky who had the idea. She wanted to get me a willow tree. And Stephen stepped in and said he would choose an ornament or decoration to go at the bottom of the tree. It was a wooden statue of a lady holding a baby. And on the box were the words, 'So Loved, So Very Loved'. With his gravestone, I just felt that it said everything we would want to say about him – but he chose those words for us. On the part at the bottom of the grave, it says, 'Jesus, remember me when you come into your Kingdom', which is from the Gospel of Luke. I don't know what Stephen found before he died, whether he'd gone anywhere on his faith journey, or whether he was even pursuing one. But I think he was searching around. He came to mass with me during the last few months. He was certainly thinking, about everything.

Mary was right, Stephen had been growing in many ways – artistically, intellectually, and spiritually. Free from the chains of addiction, he was exploring new avenues of creativity. That was one of the things that hurt the most: all that wasted talent and potential.

Mill Lane Cemetery is located on the northern outskirts of Cheadle. It opened in 1993 with long, sweeping lawns and space for around 2,000 graves. The headstones are well looked after, no doubt because those interned there all died within living memory. Visitors are greeted with a sea of colour from the flowers, the wind spinners, and the myriad other tributes that adorn each grave. At night, the solar lights shine dutifully next to those they have been left to keep company.

That cemetery became familiar a place to me. During my many visits, I often thought how this was the perfect place for Stephen to be buried – from the planes flying overhead and the train tracks to the north to the faint hum of traffic from the motorway in the distance, he was surrounded by travellers. Even the road that runs past the cemetery itself – that historic thoroughfare between Manchester and Cheshire. The road that has seen and carried so much life, from the Romans marching to *Mamucium* to the Victorian factory owners heading to the grand showrooms in the city centre, right through to the present day, with the cars, the cyclists, and the walkers. And then my thoughts shifted to the River Mersey, which sweeps along just 200 metres from the cemetery; the place this book begins – where the country and the city collide. I spent many hours there.

Although I gained some solace from the idea that Stephen's burial site was the perfect place for the natural-born traveller to rest, something still didn't sit right within me. The metaphor only stretched so far. I couldn't reconcile the fact that he was no longer there. In a state of confusion, perhaps desperation, I took to visiting his grave regularly. It was always at night. For some reason, I didn't want anyone else to be around. I would dart into the cemetery on my bike. My eyes would adjust to the blackness as the solar-powered decorations twinkled like an underwater city. So many times, I sat there, next to his grave at night, questioning how and why it came to be that he was dead. I thought about how his life was forever changed on the day he was assaulted – that unprovoked attack that led to his epilepsy. And how I hated those goddamn kids, who were still blissfully unaware of the lasting damage they had caused. It felt like such an injustice, especially as Stephen was getting his life back on track, and just as he was taking his art to the next level.

I felt lost. I no longer had my cousin to lean on. I wanted to talk to him. I thought of all the things I would have said if only I'd known that day in March would be the last.

My visits started to turn into an obsession. Now I was a hollow creature, skulking around the alleyways and the back streets, soaked in the rain. On foot or by bike, I always ended up there at Mill Lane. At times my visits were warm-spirited and talkative, as I discussed the week's events with him. Other times I was distraught, sitting cross-legged beside his grave, in floods of tears, drinking a beer and pouring one out for him. I would visit in the howling wind and the rain. His death played over and over in my mind. Gone were the days of laughter and gone were the times of joy. Drunk as hell at 2:00 am, sobbing lowly, *I miss you, I miss you*. I took my guitar to his grave, and the notes were carried away by the wind. And the bats flew around in their hundreds, and the solar lights pulsed like fireflies. At times it seemed that even the stars were weeping, but no, it was just me.

Untitled 30 (2003)
Pen and ink, chalk pastel, acrylic paint

CHAPTER TWENTY-FOUR

Rise

WHEN A PERSON dies in England, their death must be registered. This can be done in one of two ways. The first is if a doctor was in attendance during the deceased's final illness and is able to issue a medical certificate that states the cause of the death. The second, if the first cannot be achieved, is for the death to be reported to a coroner, who is tasked with finding out when, where, and how the person died. If a coroner decides that an investigation is necessary, a pathologist may carry out a post-mortem examination. Finally, if it is not possible to determine the cause of death from the post-mortem, or if the death is found to be of unnatural causes, the coroner will hold an inquest – a public hearing that aims to answer all the important questions and deliver an official verdict.

On Wednesday, October 11th, 2006, six months and one day since his body was discovered, Stephen's family gathered inside at Stockport Magistrates' Court to hear the coroner's judgement.

The group of around 18 people slowly trickled into the courthouse foyer and passed in front of three youths who were smoking in the doorway. One of them had an electronic tag around his ankle. Everyone was asked to turn in their phones to the security lockers. The rest of their belongings were placed through an airport-style scanner, and they entered the main hall through a metal detector. After waiting for a few minutes, the arrivals were called into the courtroom.

The family members took their seats in the public gallery, facing the magistrate's bench. It was a sterile and claustrophobic place, with varnished wooden panelling, harsh lighting, and no windows. A royal coat of arms hung from the wall behind the bench. Two young women sat behind the gallery – one was a stenographer, preparing to transcribe the hearing. It was unclear what the other lady was there for.

HM Coroner William Browning entered the room through a side door that connected to his chambers. The crowd rose in unison.

After stating Stephen's full name and case number, the softly-spoken official gave a brief outline of the inquest process. The hearing would establish key facts about Stephen's life, including statements from those who lived with him at the time of his death, the emergency services who were first on the scene, and medical staff who had treated him in the past.

Mary was called to the stand to confirm her son's name and other details. She remained there for the entire hearing, which allowed the coroner to refer to her with any additional questions that arose during the session.

§

The inquest sought to build a picture of Stephen's character and frame of mind during his final days. The next person to be called up was Akram, Stephen's former housemate. The coroner read aloud the statement Akram had signed the morning after Stephen's body was discovered:

WITNESS STATEMENT

Statement of: Akram AZIZ
Age: 17
Occupation: Computer Technician
Date: 11/04/2006

I am the above-named person, I live at Aberdeen Crescent, Edgeley, Stockport. I have lived here for around six months.
I have lived in the United Kingdom for around two years. I am from Iraq. I travelled to the United Kingdom when all the trouble started in my country.
When I first came to the United Kingdom I went to London. I came to Manchester to go to university. When I came to Manchester, I was homeless. I was placed in Aberdeen Crescent, Flat 2.
I am a computer technician and I work at a shop in Stockport. I normally work six days a week, from 10 o'clock in the morning until 6 o'clock at night.

I do not like it at Aberdeen Crescent because there are too many people in there, and one of the residents called Derek is always drunk.

A couple of weeks ago I saw Ste, who lives at No.3, he was inside his flat. Derek, the man from No.1, was banging on his door and shouting and swearing for him to open his door. I think it was around half past nine in the morning. I was washing just before I went to work. I did not want to get involved, I just wanted to go to work, I don't know why the man from No.1 was banging on the door of No.3.

I know the man at No.3 is called Ste, he introduced himself when he moved into the flat a few months ago.

I know he is an artist. I like his pictures. The last time I saw him was around 3 o'clock in the morning some three weeks ago. He was painting in the living room downstairs. He told me he felt sick and that's why he was painting at that time in the morning. I have not seen him since.

At around half past nine in the morning on Monday 10th April 2006, I went to work as normal. I finished at around 6 o'clock at night. I went home from work and got home at half past six, I had a shower, had something to eat, and then got a change of clothes.

At about half past seven, I went out to repair a laptop at someone's house. I replaced the hard drive.

I came home. It was dark on the landing. I opened my flat door, turned on the light inside my flat, and then heard someone call my name. I looked down the hall to see where the voice was coming from, but I couldn't see because it was too dark. I then peered into the dark. I saw it was Derek.

I said, 'DEREK', Derek said, 'I NEED HELP'. I said, 'WHAT KIND OF HELP?', Derek said, 'RING THE POLICE, AMBULANCE, AND THE CASEWORKER, SARA'.

I said, 'WHY?', Derek said, 'CAN'T YOU SEE THE PERSON IN MY HANDS? MAYBE HE'S SICK OR DEAD'. I was scared and shaking. I ran downstairs. I rang Sara and told her what Derek had said.

I then called the police on my mobile. I told them what Derek had told me. I can't remember exactly what I said to the police.

When I was on the phone with the police, I asked Derek what the problem was, he said 'MAYBE HE'S SICK, MAYBE HE'S DEAD', I told the police this. Derek was still upstairs.

I then called the ambulance and told them what had happened. A couple of minutes later the ambulance turned up. I pointed to where Derek was.

I could smell a horrible smell coming from upstairs. I think Derek had tried to bring Stephen out of his room.

The police arrived shortly afterwards.

[Signed]

A. Aziz

This was the first time the Reding family had heard Akram's account of that fateful night. And judging by the glances that were cast around the gallery, everyone was intrigued. Who was this strange Derek character? Why had no one ever heard of him before? How did he manage to get into Stephen's flat?

§

Akram provided the first in a series of statements that were written and filed immediately after the discovery of Stephen's body. The next was from another one of Stephen's housemates, Tom, who did not attend the inquest in person:

WITNESS STATEMENT

Statement of: Tom SUTTON
Age if under 18: Over 18
Date: 11/04/2006

I am the above-named person and I currently reside at Aberdeen Crescent, Edgeley, Stockport. The house is shared accommodation consisting of four individual bedrooms, a communal bathroom, toilet, kitchen, and living room.

I have previously been a resident at this accommodation, back in 2002, and then I moved to my own flat. Having been homeless for the past few months, my key worker arranged for me to move back to Aberdeen Crescent. Upon moving back, there were three other males living at the address. These males were Akram Aziz, who stayed in Room 2, Derek McBride who was in Room 1 downstairs, and a male by the name of Brian in Room 3. I moved into Room 4, which is where I have been living to this day.

Upon entering the house by the front door, the first door immediately to your left is the communal living room. Along the corridor second to the left is Room 1 and opposite this room to the right is the communal kitchen. Up the stairs and first on the left is Room 2 and next to this is the communal toilet. The corridor then bears slightly to the left and in front of you is the communal bathroom. To the right of the bathroom is my room (Room 4) and to the right of this is Room 3.

About three or four months ago, Brian moved out and a male who I already knew from around the Stockport area called Stephen Reding moved into his room. Stephen doesn't work and spends most of his time painting. Upon moving in, Stephen and I would frequently sit in the living room, either listening to music or playing chess. I don't remember him having any visitors other than his sister, who last came around about five weeks ago.

Stephen is an ex-heroin addict, and at the beginning of last month, he told me that he was on a detox programme. He later told me that he'd reduced his methadone intake to 20ml a day, and then some weeks ago he told me that he's taken himself off the methadone completely. Although Stephen may have come off the methadone, I've known for some time that he's been taking amphetamines. I've seen him take this in his drink several times, the last being about two to three weeks ago. On this occasion, Stephen was in the living room, painting. He looked very pale and not like himself at all. He told me that he had to stay awake to do his artwork. Stephen also told me about six weeks ago that the doctor had prescribed him a week's worth of sleeping tablets. Other than this, I'm not aware of Stephen being on any other medication.

The other lads that live at the house, namely Derek and Akram, are generally okay blokes. I don't spend time with either of them outside the house, but we speak when passing. Derek likes a drink and at times can be a handful. He mithers when he's had a drink, which can be irritating at times. Akram is a quiet bloke, someone whom I've never had any trouble with.

In the last three weeks, I've only seen Stephen about three times, which is unusual as I usually see him most days. The last time I saw Stephen was on Sunday the 2nd of April 2006. It was around teatime when I spoke with Stephen in the living room. He was painting at the time and looked terrible, as though he hadn't slept in days.

On Monday the 10th of April 2006, I spent most of the day at my mum's house in Wilmslow. I caught the bus back to Stockport at 6:50 pm and arrived back home at about 7:30 pm.

As I came into the house, I saw Derek in the living room. He was clearly drunk. He stunk like a brewery and was swaying on his feet. I'd recently sold a guitar for him, and he began to mither me for the money. I told him that I'd get him the money and that I would speak to him the following day when he was sober. I then went upstairs and into my room. As I passed the bathroom, I heard the bath water running, and as I went into my room, I heard Akram's door open and the bathroom door close.

At 8:30 pm that evening, there was a knock on my door. Upon opening the door, I saw Derek stood there. He was wearing a navy jacket, denim jeans, and a pale top. Derek continued going on about the money I owed him. Because I'd had enough of his mithering, I told him to go away. I shut the door and heard Derek walk along the corridor and down the stairs. I then stayed in my room watching TV.

At about 10:20 pm, Derek returned and began knocking on my door again. He continued knocking for about a minute, yet I just ignored him. Through the door, I could hear him talking to himself, yet I could not make out the words. I then heard Derek walk into the toilet and close the door. I then took this opportunity to grab my keys and coat and get out of my room. I went down the stairs and out onto the street. I then walked along Aberdeen Crescent and turned left heading towards the train station. I cut through the train station and went into *McDonald's* to use the toilet. I then walked through Grand Central, along the A6 and turned right onto Greek Street. I then walked down Castle Street and back along Aberdeen Crescent. In total, I was out walking for about three-quarters of an hour.

As I was approaching my house, I then saw the police and ambulance crew outside. I saw Akram outside and asked him what was going on. He was a little difficult to understand, yet he mentioned something about finding a body. I then walked into the house, whereupon I saw two police officers speaking to Derek. The officers then asked me to wait outside, which I did.

I then attended Stockport Police Station in the early hours of Tuesday morning, whereupon I made this statement.

[Signed]

T. Sutton

Tom's statement provides some fresh insight into the days leading up to Stephen's death. The turn of accounts continues with the first police officer at the scene:

WITNESS STATEMENT

Statement of: Rob HOUNSLOW
Age if under 18: Over 18
Occupation: Police Officer
Date: 11/04/2006

On Monday the 10th of April 2006, I was on duty in full uniform in company with PC COLEMAN. At about 2255 hours we attended a house at Aberdeen Crescent, Edgeley.

On our arrival, we were met by a paramedic Mr Jonathan BUTTERWORTH, who was already in attendance, and shown to an upstairs bedroom. The bedroom was at the end of a short landing to the right of the bathroom. The bedroom door was open, and the room was dark. On the floor, I observed the lifeless figure of a male. It appeared as though his hands were bound together. As a result of what I observed, I made the decision that there was no immediate assistance that I could offer the male, and I did not enter the room.

I immediately began to use my pocketbook to make a record of all persons present at the address, inside room one was a white male who identified himself as Mr Derek McBride, DOB 14/08/1957, Mr McBRIDE was about 5ft 9in tall with short greying hair. He was wearing a white 'Umbro' polo shirt, blue jeans, and black trainers which had two red stripes at the side. I remained outside room one and continued to speak to Mr McBride until 0035 hours on the 11th of April. At that time, I was asked by DC Sackville to seize Mr McBride's clothing. I conveyed these items to Stockport Police Station where they were sealed in police evidence bags and booked into the property system.

[Signed]

R. Hounslow

A collective gasp echoed around the courtroom. The tension was palpable. No one was to know exactly what would come to light during the inquest, but the talk of Stephen's hands being bound came as a shock. Up until this point, no one had considered the idea of foul play.

However, before those present at the inquest could dwell on the PC's astonishing statements, another account was delivered – this time from the lead investigator at the scene:

GREATER MANCHESTER POLICE

Officer Reporting: Detective Inspector Dominic WINTERS
Section: CID
Date: 12/06/2006

REPORT RE: STEPHEN REDING, DOB 01/02/1976

I report with reference to the above as follows:

At 2305hrs on Monday 10th of April 2006, I was on duty when I was informed of the report of a death at a men's hostel, located at Aberdeen Crescent, Stockport.

I attended the scene at 2340hrs in company with Detective Sergeant Stuart Fairchild. I was appraised of the situation by officers at the scene. The initial report was that a male had been found deceased in his room and there was blood present and his hands were bound.

I viewed the body of Mr Reding in situ, together with a Crime Scene Manager, Robert Graham. The deceased had been dead for some time, possibly over seven days. His body was in an advanced state of decomposition and smelt very strongly. There was blood present in the room, but it was consistent with the deceased vomiting and not as the result of a violent attack. The position of the body suggested that he had died whilst sitting on the bed and had subsequently fallen to the floor. The room was very untidy but there was no evidence of searching, and there were items of obvious value which were still in situ. The reported binding to his hand was actually skin which was sloughing from his arms as the result of decomposition. I was aware that the deceased had a poor medical history involving drug abuse and epilepsy and had been treated as recently as March 2006 for seizures.

Although the initial report suggested that the death was suspicious, I am happy that all original concerns can be reasoned away and that there was no third-party involvement in the death of Mr Reding. I am unaware of the findings of the post-mortem.

I submit the report for the attention of HM Coroner, William Browning.

[Signed]

Dominic Winters
Detective Inspector
Stockport

Detective Winters attended the inquest in person. Once his statement had been read out to the court, the coroner probed further into his colleague's suggestion that Stephen's hands had been bound. The inspector reiterated that this was not the case and that Stephen's advanced state of decomposition had resulted in his skin "sloughing" from his arms. The darkness of the bedroom and the hallway, he said, created the impression that Stephen's hands had been tied. It was also noted that there was no sign of forced entry into Stephen's flat, so it had likely been left unlocked.

Much to the family's relief, the possibility that Stephen had fallen victim to an aggressor was quickly ruled out. But this still left the vital question: How did he die? Detectives Winters and Fairchild were the ones who broke the news of Stephen's death to Mary. At the time, they said there was no evidence of drug use at Stephen's flat, and this is repeated in Detective Winter's official statement. However, given Stephen's history of both epilepsy and Class A drug use, the coroner's office obtained statements from those within the medical community who had recently treated him. The first was from his GP:

The Heatons Health Centre
3 May 2006

Dear Dr Edwards,

Re: Stephen Reding - D.O.B. 01/02/1976

Further to your letter of the 20th of April 2006, I have reviewed Stephen Reding's notes. He registered with our practice on the 17th of November 2005 and has been seen on one occasion by a locum doctor on the 26th of January 2006. I have not personally seen him.

Following a review of his notes, he has suffered from epilepsy since 1991 following an assault. When he attended the practice, he said that he had not taken any epilepsy medication for at least two years and had started to have convulsions again and had a particularly bad convulsion in December 2005. He was referred at that time for a neurological assessment at Stepping Hill Hospital. He has a history of heroin addiction and was seen by the Community Drug Team in June 2003 and followed up by them. When he was last seen by the CDT on the 28th of February 2006, he had reduced his methadone prescription to 20mls daily and was planning to stop it.

There is no record of him having received any medication since he registered at the practice in November 2005. I have enclosed copies of relevant letters from the hospital in relation to his epilepsy and his heroin addiction.

Yours sincerely,

[Signed]

Dr C. Manning

Providing additional medical information, the coroner also read out a statement from Stepping Hill Hospital, where it became apparent that Stephen had suffered a serious seizure not long before his death:

Stepping Hill Hospital
2 May 2006

Dear Dr Edwards,

Re: Stephen Joseph REDING
DOB: 01/02/1976 - DOD: 10/04/2006

I am Dr Farah Longley, Consultant in Emergency Medicine at Stepping Hill Hospital. My qualifications are MB Bchir MRCP MRCS EdA&E FFAEM.

I was the consultant on-call on the 18th of March 2006 when Stephen Reding was brought into the department at 20:30 hours. The following statement is made from the notes made at the time by the A&E Senior House Officer, who assessed and treated the patient and not from any direct knowledge or involvement with this patient.

This patient was brought by the ambulance crew having suffered from a seizure which apparently had lasted for 5-10 minutes and was witnessed by a friend. The patient had a history of epilepsy and he admitted that he had been smoking a "spliff" prior to the seizure. According to the ambulance sheet, he was not actively fitting on their arrival, had not sustained any injuries, and appeared well but complained of a headache and sore left shoulder. His Glasgow Coma Scale during the ambulance journey was 14/15. His blood sugar level was 4.3 and his blood pressure was 144/100 with a pulse of 118 and respiratory rate of 18 and equal and reactive pupils.

He was triaged at 20:30 hours with a 'yellow' triage category, and it was noticed that his anti-epileptic medication had been stopped in 2002.

At 21:25 hours he was seen by one of the Emergency Department SHOs, Dr Richard Zhang, who noted the following history. The patient had been epileptic since he was 15 years old following a head injury. He had stopped taking his medications in 2002 and had not taken any anti-epileptic medication since then. He stated that he had seizures roughly 2-3 times a year and that he was a regular cannabis user. After smoking cannabis earlier that evening, he had a seizure which lasted 5-10 minutes. He had no urinary or faecal incontinence, no tongue biting, and was uncertain as to the exact nature of the fit. He remembers waking up in the ambulance. There was no evidence that he had vomited, no evidence of a head injury, and he denied having any pain at the time of his examination. It was noticed that he had had previous shoulder dislocations through previous seizures. He denied back pain, neck pain, and shoulder pain at the time of assessment.

On examination, the patient was alert with a Glasgow Coma Score of 15/15. Before Dr Zhang was able to perform neurological observations and a physical examination, the patient decided to leave the department. He was advised to remain in the department to undergo a full assessment. However, the patient did not want to stay. The patient, therefore, did not undergo any further assessment. As he was alert and orientated, no further action was taken.

He has had no subsequent attendances to the Emergency Department after the 18th of March 2006.

Yours sincerely,

[Signed]

Dr Farah Longley
Consultant in Emergency Medicine

This was news to everyone. Not even Mary was aware that Stephen had been hospitalised on March 18th, just one week before they all went out to celebrate her brother Peter's birthday. Her mind immediately turned to the paint fumes she had smelled in Stephen's room.

"We didn't know that he had those seizures," said Mary. "We didn't know he'd been in hospital, or that he checked himself out early, nothing. He told me that he had a couple of seizures in the months leading up to his death, but not that he'd been in hospital. I just remember saying, 'Are you sure you should be painting in this bedroom, where you're sleeping?' You know what he was like: if he wanted to paint then he painted. He painted anywhere."

We will never know exactly why Stephen chose to keep these seizures to himself. However, the evidence of these medical episodes in the lead-up to his death would prove to be an important part of the inquest. So, too, was the news that he had failed to take any epilepsy medication for four years.

The coroner gave a summary of the post-mortem, a copy of which was later obtained:

POST-MORTEM EXAMINATION REPORT

Name of deceased: REDING, STEPHEN
Sex: Male
Consultant: C. MANNING
Date/Time of PM: 13.04.06 14:25
Date of Death: 10.04.06

CLINICAL HISTORY
Died within a few days of 10.4.06. History of epilepsy from age 15 following an assault. Heroin addiction from the age of 25-29. Smoked cannabis from the age of 18. On methadone programme – to come off in February. Epilepsy getting worse, and recent Stepping Hill admission with grand mal seizure. Found dead at home, body swollen and decomposing. Said to have been in bed but rolled to floor when friends assessed his condition.

EXTERNAL EXAMINATION

APPARENT AGE: 30
HEIGHT: 5' 10"
NOURISHMENT: Well nourished, 70kg
MARKS OF IDENTIFICATION: There is marked post-mortem decomposition. No evidence of any fresh venepunctures is found, although there is a suggestion of scarring in the left antecubital fossa. Tattoos are present over the neck and left shoulder.

CAUSE OF DEATH AS SHOWN BY THE EXAMINATION
Unascertained

FURTHER REMARKS
Toxicological investigation does not reveal any evidence of drug injection. It is possible that the deceased had a fatal epileptic seizure, but it is not possible to confirm this.

[Signed]

Dr D M Vaughan
MB ChB FRCPath

The news that there were no fresh marks on Stephen's arms came as a relief. However, only the toxicological report could categorically state whether he had relapsed prior to his death.

Providing the final piece in the puzzle, the report read:

Central Manchester University Hospitals

DATE: 11 May 2006
NAME OF DECEASED: Stephen Joseph REDING

TOXICOLOGICAL REPORT

Specimens for analysis were submitted on 19/04/2006 by Dr Vaughan.
The body of this 30-year-old man was reportedly found in a decomposed state. He is believed to have had a history of post-traumatic epilepsy from age 15 and misuse of drugs, for which he was on a methadone programme.

Findings, blood:

Ethanol concentration: 730 mg/l
Morphine concentration: 0 microg/l
Paracetamol concentration: 0 mg/l

[Signed]

Dr D M Vaughan
MB ChB FRCPath

Up to this point, the gallery had largely been silent. But now, amid the gasps and the hugs and the tears of gladness, an invisible weight had been lifted from the family's shoulders. It was as though everyone had been wound up like springs, and the tension was suddenly released. This was the news everyone had been hoping for. Right there on paper was the confirmation that he hadn't returned to heroin.

As he made his closing remarks, Coroner Browning repeated the findings of the post-mortem and toxicology reports, stating that drugs had not played a role in Stephen's death. He also drew attention to the fact that Stephen had neglected to take his epilepsy medication for many years and that he had a serious tonic-clonic seizure just weeks before his death. Given the evidence at hand, the coroner agreed with the pathologist's assertions by stating that, beyond all reasonable doubt, Stephen had died from an epileptic seizure. He delivered a narrative verdict at the inquest, citing natural causes as the lead factor in his death.

For the Reding family, and indeed everyone who knew Stephen, it was closure.

The family walked outside and said their brief goodbyes under a grey Stockport sky. Most of those who had attended the inquest had taken the day off work, and so they decided to reconvene at the *Red Lion* in Cheadle. An impromptu celebration of Stephen's life carried on well past sunset, as the family discussed the day's events, swapped their most cherished stories, and made several toasts to the man who had made them all so proud.

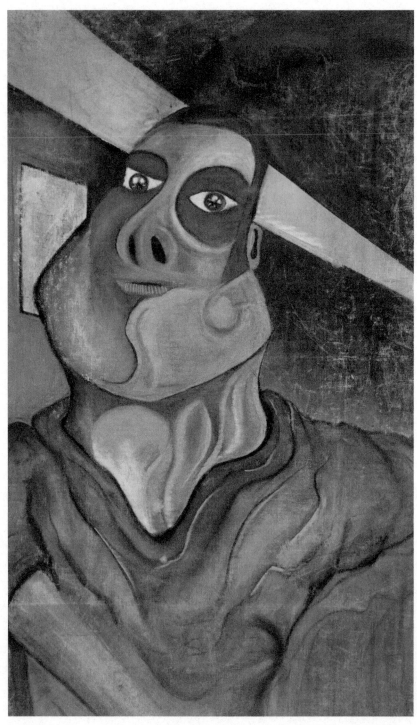

Self-portrait in a Spoon (2006)
Oil paint on canvas

Painting the Artist

I STARTED TO FORMULATE the idea to write a book about Stephen Reding in 2010. It had been four years since he had died, and the family had been moving on as best they could. But things still felt like they weren't fully resolved. The inquest had answered most of our questions, but the coroner's concluding statements only went so far. There was just so much more about my cousin's life that I felt needed to be told - all the stories, the escapades, the highs, and the lows.

Although it would be another two years until I first put pen to paper, and many more until this project was complete, I knew from the outset that this needed to be as honest an account as possible. To gloss over or omit certain elements of Stephen's life, no matter how unsavoury or incriminating, would have defeated the book's whole purpose. It was much to my relief when Mary - as I cautiously broached the subject of writing a book about her son for the first time all those years ago - agreed that this would be the only way to approach the project.

—Well, what do you think Stephen would have wanted?

She was right. Stephen wouldn't have wanted anyone to look at his life through rose-tinted glasses. He certainly didn't want anyone's sympathy.

Out of respect for the privacy of some, certain names have been changed in the telling of this tale. Out of respect for Stephen, the rest has been told as accurately as possible. And as this story comes to an end, I can only hope that this book helps him to achieve his goal of helping others overcome their own personal challenges, whatever they may be.

Mary said,

—If one person reads this book and it helps them to become free from drugs, by showing them that it can be done, then it's fulfilled its purpose. Even though Stephen died, he's a heroin recovery success story. He beat it. It was obviously a very emotional time, but when he died, my faith never faltered. If anything, it was stronger than ever. In my heart, I knew he died heroin-free.

Stephen wasn't the first person to get caught up in drugs, and he certainly won't be the last. But my lasting image of Stephen is of someone who was able to not only overcome their addictions but reclaim their identity in the face of adversity. Though his life ended far too soon, his was a story of redemption. The changes he had made over those final 12 months speak for themselves. During that time, he reconnected with everyone he was close to. Even more importantly, he was starting to find peace within himself.

I previously said that Stephen's death had filled me with anger – anger towards those lads who attacked him back in 1991, and how I blamed them for the beating that resulted in his epilepsy, the condition that took his life. If anything, Stephen's triumphant return made everything so much harder to deal with. He was on the cusp of realising his true artistic potential, and we will never know just how far his talent could have taken him. Over time, however, I came to realise that dwelling on such things was futile. Indeed, if we are to hold past events to account, then we can't ignore that penultimate beating – the attack that acted as the catalyst for Stephen's return. Things could have turned out so differently, had that troubling incident not taken place.

As the years passed by, I started to gain some perspective over my cousin's death, but I remained frustrated that he wasn't there to tell his own story. His journal was a fantastic starting point, but his notes ended abruptly. Fortunately, Stephen's friends and relatives were more than forthcoming when it came to discussing their relationship with him and helping to fill in all the gaps that muddied his narrative. I owe a great debt to everyone who has contributed to this story, especially given the emotions that were often brought to the fore in the process.

The sheer number of people who became involved in this book is a testament to the impact that Stephen had on the lives of others. I must admit that I sometimes question whether this project would have gone ahead if, for one reason or another, he had relapsed.

For Joanne, it wouldn't have mattered in the slightest.

—It wasn't even a concern for me. Even if they said he was up to his eyes in heroin, it was irrelevant. Whatever he did with his drug-taking, he did it away from the family. But he went through pain. He experienced everything, from epilepsy to self-harm through drugs. There are peaks and troughs. He explored the full range of what anybody could do on this planet, within their own capacity. I'm not talking about things that money can buy. I'm talking about the things someone can do with their body. And yet, through all of this, he was so centred. He knew how much we loved him, and he always felt as if he had let us down. On that last day when we all went for a walk, he said, 'Do you know, I'm the eldest in the family? I feel as if I should be married, and I should have children. I feel I should be able to drive a car and have a house'. And I just remember looking at him and saying, 'Why do you need that? Why do you think you need it?' And he laughed, he said, 'I don't know, really. I just wanted to hear what you were going to say'. I said, 'We have no expectation of you, we just love you, and we just want you to be here'. To this day, I have never really felt that he has died, because he's still so alive. And that's beautiful. That is a beautiful thing. That is a gift.

§

During my research for this book, I came across several previously unknown pieces of information relating to Stephen, all of which help to build a more complete picture of his life. One weekend, in particular, gave rise to numerous revelations. But first, some background is needed:

In the autumn of 2006, Mary and her daughter Becky were at a supermarket in Cheadle Heath. They were packing bags to raise money for the Lourdes group. Out of the corner of her eye, Mary saw Stephen's biological father at one of the checkout counters.

—I just went over to him and his partner, and said, 'I don't know if you are aware, but Stephen's passed away'. His partner left us alone to have a chat. And he said, yes, he knew. He had seen Stephen's name in the paper. We had a nice chat, and I said he was buried at Mill Lane. When I went to visit Stephen a few weeks later, there was a lovely plant in a pot by his grave. It said, 'Always loved, never forgotten'. That gesture was lovely to me.

This brings us to the weekend when several missing pieces came together. The reader may recall that there were two women in the courtroom during the inquest, one of whom was a stenographer. When Mary later told me that Stephen's biological father had seen his name in the newspaper, an alarm bell went off in my head: the other woman was a journalist.

On an overcast Friday, I took a train from Manchester to Stockport and walked to the heritage library. I had previously visited the library on three separate occasions, scouring the local newspaper archives for Stephen's name. With a rough timeline in mind as to when he was arrested, I limited my searches to 2005. If only I'd thought to cast the net wider, because after taking my seat at the microfilm reader once again, I soon discovered another article from the following year:

Epileptic found dead in his flat

A STOCKPORT artist died from an epileptic fit in his Edgeley flat, an inquest heard.

Stephen Reding had stopped taking his medication two years before his death despite the fact he still suffered from seizures.

In March he was taken to hospital after a fit but he discharged himself before a full assessment was made.

Shortly after Christmas Mr Reding, aged 30, moved into a sheltered

accommodation on Aberdeen
Crescent but had appeared unwell in
the weeks before his death.
On April 10 a housemate, Akram Aziz,
found another resident standing
near Mr Reding's room calling for help.
Police and paramedics were called
and found Mr Reding's body on the
floor of his room.
A post-mortem revealed Mr Reding to
be in a severe state of decomposure.
Pathologist David Vaughan said he
carried out extensive tests but failed
to discover a definite cause of death.
Coroner William Browning returned a ver
-dict of natural causes.[13]

- *Stockport Express*, October 18th, 2006

It's difficult to imagine how any press coverage relating to Stephen's death went unnoticed, particularly given the size of his family. But for some reason, this 150-word article had passed everyone by. Reading this short piece for the first time filled me with emotion. It was moving to note that Stephen was qualified by the nouns 'artist' and 'epileptic' – two simple terms that shaped his entire life.

By the time I left the library, it had started to rain. I walked past the art gallery, where I had met Stephen for the final time six years earlier, and the drizzle turned into a downpour. I kept on walking, retracing our steps to arrive at Aberdeen Crescent. I looked up to see the rain bouncing against his window.

Later that day, I visited Mary in Cheadle Heath where, over a cup of coffee, I showed her the newspaper article that I had found. Our conversation turned to Stephen's possessions. My aunt initially set me up for disappointment when she said,

—I must admit that I threw some stuff away after he died. I wish I hadn't - I would have given them to you. I just wasn't in the right state of mind.

Before I could dwell on these lost items, however, my worries disappeared as Mary brought down the first of three large storage boxes that were full of Stephen's belongings. She also presented me with several art folios and dozens of loose canvases and sketches.

—If you're visiting all weekend, I might as well just run you back with all of this and you can go through it in your own time.

That evening, I scattered the contents of the boxes onto the living room floor. Camera in hand, I started to catalogue his paintings and put the documents in order. Mary had given me everything. There were countless personal items, including notebooks, letters, and photographs. There were samples of his greeting cards - small ones in elegant white boxes with a red bow. They still smelled new. Also included in the collection of artefacts were the hundreds of sympathy cards and letters received by the Reding family following Stephen's death. Wrapped in tissue paper and placed in a small plastic box were the ring and chain Stephen had been wearing when he died.

While the contents of these boxes would prove to be instrumental to my research, one item stood out over everything else. This was not a photograph or a letter, nor a piece of art. It was a simple, A4 week-to-view diary. I initially mistook it for another of Stephen's sketchbooks, as it didn't have a cover like most other diaries. It was made from thin, recycled cardboard, like an exercise book, with white masking tape running down the spine - a quick repair job to keep the whole thing from falling apart.

Unassuming as this document may be, this diary is one of the most valuable things Stephen left behind, perhaps even more so than his journal, for it offers clear evidence that he was getting his life back on track. Here we see a man tackling his responsibilities head-on and getting things done, in so many ways - from his art and relationships to his personal well-being and intellectual growth.

The start of the diary coincides with when Stephen moved into his flat in January 2006. And thereafter, nearly every day bears a handwritten entry of some description. *Sign for lease for flat. Meet Sara. Contact Auntie Irene and Uncle Geoff. Nana and Grandpa. Ask Mum about the table! Send letters and thank you cards to family. Books: Art history, English lit, lang, teacher training. Relapse prevention group. Nicholas. Make payment Post Office. Look after Jamie – afternoon. Contact Andy. Payment, £170 bank. Inform doctors of seizures. Make a start on the selection of sketches. Doctor Royal, fracture clinic. GET UP EARLY. Link Work session. Go running, three miles. Library, 10 books!*

The final entry in Stephen's diary was on Saturday, March 11th, 2006. *Hook up with James.* After that, the pages were blank. But even though the memos came to an impromptu end, those two-and-a-half months' worth of entries meant so much more to me than the results of any toxicology report. The diary presents a real-time narrative of someone who was on their way to becoming the very best version of himself.

As I flicked through the pages of the diary, two pieces of paper fell onto the floor. The first was a thin greeting card with my address written on it, along with the words 'Send to James ASAP'. The other was an unassuming checklist of things to do. But there, written in the margin, were the words, 'Write your new book'. This was enough for me to know that Stephen wanted his story to be told.

Finally, everything seemed so clear. My research was almost complete.

§

I write these final words on December 31st, 2022. Ten years is a long time to have spent on any endeavour, and in all honesty, I don't know how I'm going to feel now that the project is complete. It has been with me for so long, but now it is time for Stephen's story to be sent out into the world.

It has been a long journey, but in writing this book, I feel that I have got to know Stephen better than I ever did when he was alive. Ultimately, as I pass this tale to others, I would urge the reader not to think of his story as a tragedy. When we think of Stephen and look back on all those cherished times, please know that his family is celebrating, not mourning. This may not be a fairy tale ending, but Stephen's death doesn't hurt so much when you realise what he found: Life.

As the years passed, I no longer felt the need to visit Stephen's grave so often. I realised that he would always be right here with me. Of course, we all still miss him dearly. And there are still times when I catch myself in certain situations asking, 'What would Ste do?' But whenever I feel downtrodden, or whenever life is getting the better of me, I simply turn to his *Self-portrait in a Spoon* – the painting that frames this chapter. When I look at that painting, I see someone looking resolutely to the future with life in his eyes, saying, 'Here I am! It's me! Let's go!'

The hope that pours through that painting is infectious.

Untitled 25 (2002)
Pen and ink, watercolour

Untitled 26 (2002)
Acrylic paint, oil pastel

Stephen Joseph Reding
1976–2006

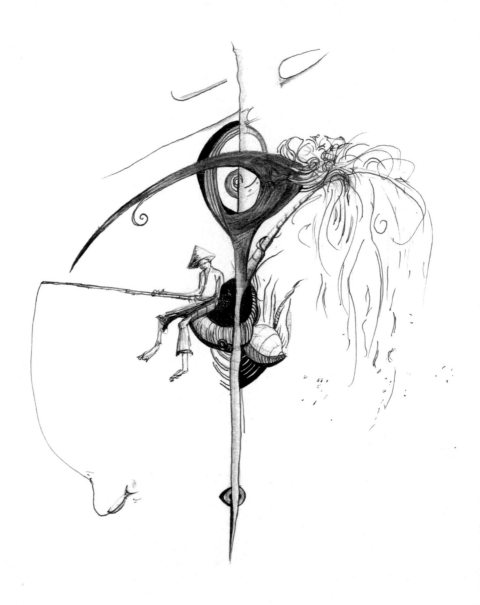

Untitled 14 (2001)
Pencil

End Notes

[1] A poem at the confluence of the River Tame and the River Goyt in Stockport, the birthplace of the River Mersey. Public domain.

[2] Manchester Evening News, '*Killer Cold Strikes the Old Folk*' (Saturday, January 31st, 1976, p1); '*Cold Dole Workers Walk Out*' (Monday, January 26, 1976, p1); '*Too Cold For School (Overcoat Kids Told to Stay at Home)*' (Saturday, January 31st, 1976, p5).

[3] Data from the Epilepsy Research UK website (2022), "There are over 600,000 people in the UK with a known diagnosis of epilepsy – That's about one in 103 people". Reproduced with kind permission from Epilepsy Research UK.

[4] Information on traumatic brain injuries taken from the Epilepsy Foundation of America website (2022). Reproduced with kind permission from the US non-profit.

[5] Iyer, Pico, *Why we travel*, first delivered in a lecture at the Smithsonian in 1996 and reprinted in Salon.com in 2000. Extract reproduced with the kind permission of the author.

[6] Data from *Comparative epidemiology of dependence on tobacco, alcohol, controlled substances, and inhalants: Basic findings from the National Comorbidity Survey* (1994), p251, Table 2, 'Estimated Prevalence of Extramedical Use and Dependence in Total Study Population and Lifetime Dependence Among Users'. Heroin was given an estimated dependency rate of 23.1%.

[7] Data from the UK government report, *Adult Substance Misuse Treatment Statistics 2020 to 2021*, "The number of people in treatment for opiate use was very similar to last year (going up slightly from 140,599 to 140,863)".

[8] Real name unknown. Any resemblance to a real person, living or dead, by name or location, is purely coincidental.

[9] Dudgeon, David, *Millennium Mileposts* (1999). Poem reproduced with the kind permission of the author.

[10] Stockport Express, '*In the Dock*', Wednesday, June 8th, 2005, p4. Article reproduced with the kind permission of Stockport Express/Reach Plc.

[11] Parry, Sir Edward Abbott, *What the Judge Saw: Being Twenty-Five Years in Manchester By One Who Has Done It* (1912). Public domain.

[12] Walker, James, *Time is Flying* (2006).
https://james-walker.bandcamp.com/album/time-is-flying

[13] Stockport Express, '*Epileptic found dead in his flat*', Wednesday, October 18th, 2006, p2. Article reproduced with the kind permission of Stockport Express/Reach Plc.

Acknowledgements

This book would not have been possible without the love and encouragement of my wife and best friend, Elsa. Thank you for your unwavering patience, guidance, and support. I love you.

Thank you to all on the production team who were crucial to the completion of this project: Katarina Nskvsky for the fantastic front cover, Dawn Black for the layout design work, Jess Haworth for final copy checks, and the many others who lent their thoughts, advice, and proofreading skills. Special thanks to Ian Harding for the studio photography work and image editing.

I am grateful to the more than 80 individuals, organisations, and charities who kindly offered their time, expertise, and experience to this book. This, of course, includes everyone in Stephen's family, and all his friends and loved ones who are featured in this story. Thank you for finding the strength to talk about past events and trusting me to handle this project with care; not only have you brought Stephen's story to life, but I also hope your contributions will help draw attention to the important issues of epilepsy and addiction.

Special thanks to the non-profits Epilepsy Research UK and the Epilepsy Foundation of America, who allowed me to include their research data, along with Professor Matthew Walker at University College London's Queen Square Institute of Neurology for his candid insight. I would like to extend this thanks to all the charities, research institutes, and healthcare professionals who are working tirelessly to improve the lives of people with epilepsy, along with the many other vital organisations that are tackling homelessness and helping vulnerable people find secure accommodation across the UK.

Thank you to writers Pico Iyer and David Dudgeon, who kindly allowed me to cite their work in this book, along with the Reach Plc licensing team for allowing me to include the newspaper extracts. Thank you to the Manchester Central and Stockport library staff for always pointing me in the right direction.

Thank you to my mum and my sister for always being there. And thank you to Mary. For everything.

- James Walker, 2023

Ko Samui (2000)
Pen and ink, watercolour

About the Author

James Walker is an editor, journalist, and copywriter from Manchester, England. This is his first book.

For more information, visit **paintingtheartist.com**.

If you enjoyed reading this book, please consider leaving a review online.

Your review will help this story reach as many people as possible.

Please leave a review wherever you purchased HIT: Once Upon a Field.